Stop the World, I Want to Get Off...

Stop the World, I Want to Get Off...

Unpublished Letters to
The Daily Telegraph

EDITED BY
IAIN HOLLINGSHEAD

Aurum
Press

Quarto is the authority on a wide range of topics.

Quarto educates, entertains and enriches the lives of
our readers—enthusiasts and lovers of hands-on living.

www.QuartoKnows.com

First published 2016 by
Aurum Press Ltd
74–77 White Lion Street
London N1 9PF

A catalogue record for this book is available from the British Library.

ISBN 978 1 78131 545 3
eISBN 978 1 78131 549 1

10 9 8 7 6 5 4 3 2 1

2020 2019 2018 2017 2016

Typeset in Mrs Eaves by SX Composing DTP, Rayleigh, Essex

Printed and bound in Great Britain by CPI Group (UK) Ltd, Croydon, CR0 4YY

FSC
www.fsc.org
MIX
Paper from
responsible sources
FSC® C020471

SIR – My garden is being overrun by slugs in the wet weather. Is there anything that will divert them away from my plants?

As a non-gardener I am not really interested in the answer; I just want to get the *Telegraph* letters back on track after the EU referendum.

Timothy Lee
Kenilworth, Warwickshire

CONTENTS

CONTENTS

INTRODUCTION

Does life go on after Bowie, Brexit and *Downton Abbey*? Looking back through the seven previous introductions to the books in this series, I notice that I have said on more than one occasion that it has been a busy and eventful year for *Telegraph* letter writers. Now, of course, I wish I had kept my powder dry for 2016. A week used to be a long time in politics; at times this year an hour has seemed an aeon. Stalwart contributors to the letters page discovered that a pithy opinion dashed off during breakfast was out of date by elevenses. To give you a sense of the scale of change, back at Easter we received a flippant letter (ploughing the familiar furrow that the best way to be published by the editor is to flatter the editor), suggesting that the country would be better run by *Telegraph* journalists than by career politicians. One of the letter's more ridiculous suggestions included the appointment of Boris Johnson as Foreign Secretary. No doubt it remained unpublished as it was seen as far too far-fetched, even as a joke.

Humour has been in short supply in the news this year, so I hope you find the wicked wit of *Telegraph* letter writers a welcome tonic. Competition to appear in these pages has been especially fierce: in the immediate aftermath of the Brexit vote, the newspaper received over 1,000 letters every day, a figure unparalleled since the MPs' expenses scandal. Why, they wondered, couldn't the EU operate freedom of movement along similar lines to a Waitrose car park? Why wasn't *The Archers* as gripping as the Westminster soap opera? Less whimsically, the readers were on particularly fine form during the referendum campaign itself, treating the twin imposters of Project Fear and the Be-Leavers with equal disdain. Indeed, I would venture that there is more genuine insight in these pages than we saw in any number of televised debates or learned commentaries (although perhaps you will be grateful that I have spared you the half-dozen correspondents who attempted a variation on Hamlet's soliloquy: "To Leave or Not to Leave?").

Of course, while Brexit has dominated the news agenda, there has been far more to the year than politics. *Telegraph* correspondents have been on hand to provide their own refreshing take on every event under the sun, whether attempting to read the handwriting on striking doctors' placards or suggesting a new cockney rhyming slang in honour of Andy Murray's second Wimbledon victory. Roy Hodgson, Sir John Chilcot, David Cameron, Chris Evans and Lord Grantham have all been shown out of the tradesman's entrance with varying degrees of sadness, making way for the likes of Donald Trump and Boaty McBoatface. Add to this the readers' perennial off-beat thoughts on everything from sex to gardening; the perils of growing old, fat, drunk and unfashionable; the pain of broadcasters' mangling of the English language; the cross words of puzzle enthusiasts; and the disaster that ensued when one man gave up his seat on the London Underground for a blind person – and you have, I hope, a very readable review of the year, in all its dubious glory.

It is always such a pleasure to pick up my red pen and see what the readers have come up with over the year. As ever, my grateful thanks to all our loyal correspondents, as well as to everyone at Aurum and the *Telegraph*, in particular Kate Moore on the letters desk, who mined mountains of missives with consummate skill, a keen eye and a ready wit. However mad the world might seem, however tempted one might be to hop off for a while, hopefully this collection is a reminder that the ride taken in good company is always a fascinating one.

Iain Hollingshead
London SE22

FAMILY LIFE AND TRIBULATIONS

SEASONS' GREETINGS PILE

SIR — I have received a lengthy round-robin Christmas message from someone called Peg. I haven't a clue who she is, but if she reads the *Telegraph,* could I wish her a rapid recovery from her recent haemorrhoid operation.

Ian McDougle
Farnham Common, Buckinghamshire

SIR — We have received an unsigned Christmas card which says: "Hope you are well. I just keep taking the tablets."

As we are now in an older age group, this criterion covers about 98 per cent of our acquaintances. I guess we will just have to wait until next Christmas to find out if the tablets are still working.

Wendy Strathdee
Burnham, Buckinghamshire

SIR — I have thought Christmas to be overrated for more years than I care to remember, but last night really brought me to breaking point. Why do frying pans not come ready gift-wrapped?

Tim Bradbury
Northwich, Cheshire

SIR — When walking around Bath last Christmas I came across a health food shop advertising just the present for the person who has everything: "Colonic irrigation; Gift vouchers available."

Nigel Day
Frome, Somerset

SIR – The RSPCA is telling people not to dress up their dogs at Christmas as it leaves them scared, worried and unable to express themselves. Now they know how it feels to get a novelty Christmas jumper.

P.C.
Northampton

SIR – It is so unfair to have a birthday at Christmas. I would like to suggest a ban on all sexual activity from, say, March 15 to March 31.

Diana Whiteside
Berkhamsted, Hertfordshire

DAILY DELIGHTS

SIR – At the age of 76 I am delighted to learn from your newspaper that a daily orgasm could significantly reduce my chances of developing prostate cancer. Would two a day improve my odds further, or does the law of diminishing returns apply?

M.G.P.
Northwood, Middlesex

SIR – Now they tell us!

Robert Hood-Wright (in receipt of Winter Fuel Allowance)
Nanstallon, Cornwall

SIR — My husband, on learning from *The Daily Telegraph*
that happily married couples made love just once a week,
wistfully commented: "Please could we be an unhappily
married couple?"

Susan Jones
Halesowen, West Midlands

SIR — It was somewhat unsettling to read that cat owners
have sex twice a week and dog owners three times a week. At
one time I owned five dogs and eight cats. When I walked
the dogs I was met with cheerful waves from passers-by. Now
I'm rather embarrassed at what they might have been smiling
about.

Lesley Thompson
Lavenham, Suffolk

SIR — I see that wolf-whistling is to be treated as a hate crime
by Nottinghamshire Police.
   When I was nine months pregnant with my daughter, I
was wolf-whistled in the street by a passing lorry driver.
   It made my day. I felt less like an elephant and more like
a human being.

Jill Gibb
Deeping St James, Lincolnshire

SIR — My first wife would turn around and go back for
seconds if she heard a wolf-whistle.

C.W.
Alderminster, Warwickshire

SIR – Your correspondent's romantic hideaway sleeping three reminds me of the rules of a Chinese hotel I stayed in on business back in the 1980s. Among the many banned items on the list in the room were "wrestling" and "lascivious thoughts".

That really put paid to my down-time.

David Brown
Lavenham, Suffolk

SIR – On a recent cruise I was talking to a spritely old widow lady who asked: "What does SAGA stand for?"

Jokingly, I replied, "Sex and Games for the Aged."

Wistfully she murmured, "If only."

Terry Morrell
Willerby, East Yorkshire

SIR – I am 80, a widow, and in the process of shortening some of my clothes because my boyfriend says I have good legs.

D.P.
Sutton Coldfield, West Midlands

SIR – A very proper old lady of my acquaintance was heard to say, some years ago now, "I do like bananas. But I can't eat them."

The alternative uses have been the subject of much speculation ever since.

Pete Townsend
Bristol

SIR — Now that oysters are the same price as cod fish fingers, how are we to choose which of the two aphrodisiacs to serve for a given romantic encounter?

Neil Sewell-Rutter
Oxford

SIR — If a regular glass of red wine and plenty of fruit are supposed to improve one's sex life in middle age, how is it that the only benefit I have gained is a painful case of gout?

David Jepson
Derby

SIR — The claim made for the benefits of a diet rich in red wine and fruit is rash. After copious amounts of Shiraz during the festive period and liberal use of my new zappy juicer I have come out in urticaria.

This look will not drive anything, especially sex — unless you like your men well red.

David Parker
Rhayader, Powys

SIR — You report that Britain's oldest tree, the Fortingall Yew in Perthshire, appears to be undergoing a sex change as it is developing the red berries associated with the female yew. As I approach my 62nd year, I too am developing red berries. Should I be worried?

Alistair Donald
Stirling

SIR – Regarding your article about ogling rugby players I have to confess that, even at the advanced age of 75, I still like to see a nice pair of shoulders and strong thighs. My first thought, though, on seeing these muscular heroes is always: Thank goodness I don't have to feed them.

Lois Quinn
Coventry

TRANSUBSTANTIATION

SIR – My wife eats twice as much as I do, yet she is slim and I am overweight. I put it down to trans fats: she transfers her fat to me each night while I am asleep.

Tony Cowan
Elgin, Moray

SIR – Paul Hollywood says that losing weight is not rocket science. He's right: it's far more difficult.

Richard Amies
Weybourne, Norfolk

SIR – With the obesity problem worsening every day, Squeezy Belly Alley in Port Isaac seems aptly named.

Jane Cullinan
Padstow, Cornwall

SIR – With the proposed introduction of a sugar tax, will the substitution of alternative sweeteners by soft drink companies be regarded as tax evasion?

James Nuthall
Epsom, Surrey

SIR – Maybe the "civilised" world is getting its comeback. After our "heroes" Drake, Raleigh etc. brought back sugar and tobacco, along with slaves, we now find ourselves dying from smoking-related diseases and obese and ill from too much sugar.

Just desserts?

Ann Baker
Wilcove, Cornwall

SIR – As far as I recall I should now be drinking each day: three glasses of fruit juice; three cups of coffee; and three to five cups of tea, having fried my breakfast eggs and bacon in butter.

Is this all correct or should I be eating a portion of fish twice a week to improve my memory?

Captain Roger Gorst RN (retd)
Pucklechurch, Gloucestershire

SIR – It would appear that, whatever I eat or do not eat, I shall still one day die. In the meantime, l shall continue to eat sausages; it is unthinkable for an Englishman not to do so.

Dr Bertie Dockerill
Shildon, Co Durham

SIR — In claiming that tea is Britain's national drink, your writer might care to know the real reason. When a French friend of mine was asked why the British drink so much tea, he gave the ready reply: "Have you tasted their coffee?"

Professor Jack Mahoney
Oxford

SIR — Your correspondent suggests that food packaging should tell consumers how much exercise is needed to burn off the calories in the product. Please could it also include the number of calories that are burned when trying to open said packaging.

Lynne Waldron
Woolavington, Somerset

SIR — In my Christmas stocking was a little cutting tool, "useful for opening difficult plastic packages". Guess what it was packaged in.

Peter Fineman
Mere, Wiltshire

DIY SPACEWALK

SIR — I am a great admirer of Major Tim Peake's achievements — even more so after viewing your front-page photo of him preparing for a spacewalk. Unlike my husband he appears to be reading the instructions before attempting the task.

Marianne Charlesworth
Old Chatton, Norfolk

SIR – My husband, aged 70, recently purchased a drill. He has never owned one or used one. The last 48 hours have been a revelation. Now if I could just persuade him to eat cheese, life would be perfect.

Rosemary Rowley-Wootton
Kidderminster, Worcestershire

SIR – Nicola Sturgeon approaches a referendum in a similar style to my doomed DIY projects: keen to instigate and always dissatisfied with the end result.

Paul Coakes
Droitwich, Worcestershire

SIR – I was amazed to learn that Sarah Vine has the time and patience to send her husband, Michael Gove, an email with her advice. Don't they talk to each other? I wish my bride of 50 years would do the same, but she claims she can't shout in an email, nor ensure that I obey.

Peter Froggatt
Dorking, Surrey

SIR – I find that a to-do list, strategically placed for my husband to see, has far more effect than actually asking him several times in person. The satisfaction he feels as he crosses each job off the list is nothing compared to mine as I think of yet another one to add to the bottom.

Catherine Kidson
Bradfield, Berkshire

SIR – Men's opportunities to show their prowess at home have been reduced to cooking on charcoal barbecues and fixing recalcitrant Christmas tree lights. Barbecues are now almost universally heated by gas, while cranky Christmas tree lights have been replaced by highly reliable LEDs.

I am just going out to my shed and I may be some time.

Jos Binns
Camerton, Somerset

TILL DEATH US DO PART

SIR – I read with dismay the conclusions by university psychologists that men have a shorter life expectancy because they are less likely to seek medical advice.

Married men die before their wives because they want to.

Leonard Gold
London WC2

SIR – Having committed some minor infringement, I recently said to my wife that she really should divorce me, whereupon she replied that she wouldn't do that as I "hadn't suffered enough yet".

After 56 years of marriage, I am hopeful that my sentence will not be commuted.

Dr John Leane
Beaconsfield, Buckinghamshire

SIR – My wife recently used the expression "from the get-go". Is this grounds for divorce?

Andrew Bebbington
Cheadle, Cheshire

SIR — At the end of each day I am considering asking my wife to complete a short survey. Questions would include: "How did I do today?" and "Would you recommend me to relatives and friends?"

Peter Colson
Writtle, Essex

SIR — Today is our 45th wedding anniversary. I didn't receive the traditional sapphire associated with this achievement. However, I did get a garden bench with an engraved brass plaque which read: "1971–2016: Sapphire so Good".

Need I say more?

G.L.
Tadworth, Surrey

SIR — In honour of Mother's Day, I would like to chronicle the various names by which my wife has been known over the years: Moussaka for a while; then The Mother Ship; and now she is known as Dad's Tax Loophole.

Keith Macpherson
Houston, Renfrewshire

THE AGE INDEX

SIR — In an attempt to pre-empt any ageing of my brain I have recently adopted a simple exercise plan based on movements in the FTSE100 Index. I add the daily opening and closing prices together, convert that figure into steps and off I go with my dog.

I'm hoping that when the markets reopen after Easter there will be cause for a much more challenging distance to be covered. My dog agrees with me.

Lady Vanessa Watson
Little Waltham, Essex

SIR – You report that playing online brain games significantly improves memory in the over-fifties. My attempt to download this game was thwarted when I couldn't remember my password.

George Halford
London SW14

SIR – As an ageing hearing aid wearer, your two headlines today: "Hearing aid cuts hastening mental decline"; and "Learn a language to ward off dementia" put me in a quandary. Do I hedge my bets and choose Sign Language?

Owen Hay
Stanway, Essex

SIR – I am reminded of my late father who, upon finding in later years that the sound on his television was not so clear, discovered that holding a scallop shell to the ear offered significant amplification.

A later modification allowed for an elastic band to be looped over the ear to trap the scallop shell (or latterly shells) in place, thus leaving the hands free.

Robert Rowland
Evesham, Worcestershire

SIR — Some years ago, when my recently divorced mother moved to South London, her widowed neighbour asked if she would like to come to Ascot with him. She was delighted to accept, and turned up for the trip wearing her best frock and a new hat.

The neighbour complimented her, saying, "My, you look lovely."

"Well, I want to look my best for Ascot," she replied.

"No, no, I said Asda," he said, somewhat embarrassed.

He had had in mind a shopping trip, and my dear mother was somewhat hard of hearing.

Sadly, she died not long afterwards, and we buried her in Putney Vale cemetery, ironically adjacent to the same supermarket. I suggested putting "Gone to Ascot" on the tombstone, but was overruled by my unamused family.

A.D.
Burton upon Trent, Staffordshire

SIR — After reading your obituaries for many years, I finally find that, in today's newspaper, I am older than all three who are honoured.

Is this an achievement?

Rev Michael A. Bentley (age 81 and one twelfth)
Bracknell, Berkshire

SIR — Definition of aged: when your children are discussing their retirement plans with each other.

Ken Wells
Bognor Regis, West Sussex

SIR – I am rather worried by your report that regular churchgoers live longer. I am Jewish.

P.F.
Mere, Wiltshire

SIR – Some years ago, when my father was approaching 80, he needed a new pair of shoes. He made his selection at the shop and asked if the shoes would wear well.

He was a little hurt when the young assistant replied: "Oh yes, they'll see you out."

Peter Gibbs
Taunton, Somerset

SIR – I was delighted when, during a medical check-up following my recent 76th birthday, the doctor told me that I was in good shape for my age.

I was not so pleased when he added: "The only thing that gives it away is your face."

Robert Readman
Bournemouth, Dorset

SIR – As an interested party, I note with some concern the number of men who are dying in their seventies. I shall be glad when I turn 80 and the danger is averted.

Roy Bailey
Great Shefford, Berkshire

SIR – Dame Judy Dench has had a tattoo to celebrate her 81st birthday. I can only say that she will probably come to regret it when she grows old.

Peter Bailey
Cardiff

SIR – Your reporter thinks old people are invisible here in the UK. She should come to Swindon: people are forever telling me to get out of the way.

Jim Brooks
Stanton Fitzwarren, Wiltshire

SIR – Your paper urges employers not to consign workers in their seventies to their rocking chairs.

When I was in my eighties I was employed in the call centre of a housing association. Most of my co-workers were young married women.

Once I was instructed to attend a seminar organised by my employers on "Harassment at Work". Two ex-policemen lectured us at length and then asked the attendees in turn whether they had experienced harassment.

I explained that I had only been in my present position for a short time and had not experienced any sexual harassment to date, but that I was living in hope.

Sid Davies
Bramhall, Cheshire

SIR – I watched with awe the magnificently athletic Angela Rippon presenting *How to Stay Young*, which seeks to promote a healthy lifestyle for the elderly. One of the "tests for suppleness and core strength" involved lowering oneself to the floor from a standing position and standing up again without using one's arms.

I attempted this in the privacy of my own bedroom and managed to lower myself to a cross-legged (and cross-eyed) position on the floor. Sadly, when I attempted to stand up again, I lost my balance and careered backwards into a very substantial solid oak dressing table. I fractured my leg in two places and cracked three ribs.

Ken Grimrod-Smythe
Ingbirchworth, South Yorkshire

SIR — I could not help but be impressed by your photograph of the Rolling Stones. Nature has been kind to these septuagenarians: not an ounce of fat on any of them; they all have a great head of hair; and they look better than most of the old buffers in my golf club living a healthy life in the Algarve sunshine.

There must be something in all that sex, drugs and rock 'n' roll after all.

Jane Rackham
Almancil, Portugal

SIR — My wife is deaf and we had the following conversation recently:

"Aren't you playing golf this morning?"
"No, I'm not. There is a trolley ban."
"What?"
"THERE IS A TROLLEY BAN."
"How come you can't play golf because of the Taliban?"

K.H.
Bollington, Cheshire

GOLF COURSE BITCHES

SIR — Muirfield's decision not to allow women members comes as no surprise to me. In the late 1950s my then fiancée took me to Preswick, his all-male Scottish club, and enquired about paying a green fee.

"It's a ten shilling fine to take a dog around the course but nothing for a woman," came the dour reply.

My status of being lower than a dog prepared me well for 55 years of marriage, where I have sometimes had to take second place to a series of black Labrador bitches.

Liz Young
Long Marston, Hertfordshire

SIR — Many years ago, as a US Marine Corps Doctor attached to the Grenadier Guards, I remember a young titled officer being asked by a Scottish visitor to the regiment if he was a golfer.

He recoiled in visible horror and replied: "My father taught me that a golf club was merely a Sergeants' Mess with Jaguars."

Dr Geoffrey Francis
Fort Lauderdale, Florida, USA

SIR — As the length of my drives has become a problem, I have been wondering if it is too late in life to self-define as a lady golfer and play off their tees. I am in the throes of composing a letter to my club, the R&A. As it now admits ladies it should really only be a question of changing locker-rooms.

Rev Dr John Cameron
St Andrews, Fife

THE DRONE SEASON

SIR – Your correspondents are wondering how to discourage drones. Just add them to the "shooting list", as with game. Any game over my land is mine to shoot. There will be no need for seasons as drones are not known to breed.

What shot size would be recommended?

Ian Clark
London SE8

SIR – Having recently experienced a drone hovering over the roof windows of my large, open-plan kitchen, I too am worried about the invasion of privacy.

The only consolation was the satisfaction that, on looking at any recorded footage, the operator might be shocked to see my teenage son, dressed in in a black curly wig and 46-inch bell-bottom trousers, preparing for a 1970s fancy-dress party by throwing *Saturday Night Fever* moves with great gusto, while his mother stuck two fingers up at the drone and shouted obscenities at the drone out of the back door.

I hope I adequately demonstrated the behaviour of the real housewives of Cheshire.

Stella Currie
Bramhall, Cheshire

SIR – As a member of The Drones Club, Bertie Wooster was clearly well ahead of his time.

Tony Greenham
Sutton, Cheshire

UNHAPPY SHOPPERS

SIR – Your photograph depicts scores of people on Oxford Street participating in the Boxing Day sales, presumably with a view to saving money or enjoying the experience in some other way which is lost on many of us. What does it tell us about the modern world that every single one of them looks so unhappy?

Sam Kelly
Dobcross, Lancashire

SIR – I saw a photograph of a mass of unkempt and unhappy people pressed against the door of a building. I assumed they were refugees desperate for registration.
On reading the caption it said they were waiting to purchase the latest iPhone.

Q.D. McGill
Sutton Coldfield, West Midlands

SIR – If only other stores would follow Marks & Spencer's music ban I could dispense with my earplugs – and my mortified daughter would come shopping with me again. She has refused to do so since 2008 when I called a shop manager outside and asked to be served on the pavement.

Lesley Thompson
Lavenham, Suffolk

SIR – Last year my partner split the seam in her trousers while having to bend down very low to look at the underwear in BHS. In her disgust she put a curse on them. Look what has happened since.

D.G.
Norwich

SIR — It has occurred to me that if the Duchess of Cambridge had been photographed wearing an outfit from BHS perhaps it might have saved the company.

Stephen Ennis
Thames Ditton, Surrey

DEDICATED FAULTFINDERS OF FASHION

SIR — Could the men's clothes shown in the *Telegraph* this week explain why my wife finds it difficult to find curtain material nowadays?

Bruce Cochrane
Bridge of Allan, Stirlingshire

SIR — Finally, after 78 years, I have reached the pinnacle of fashion. The surgical stockings I am wearing after a recent operation match the stockings of the Gucci girl on page 11 of yesterday's *Telegraph*.

Margaret Baker
Poole, Dorset

SIR — Proof of my husband's reluctance to buy new clothes was shown when he opened a Father's Day card showing a picture of him and our then five-year-old daughter. He is wearing a blue and white check shirt which he still wears regularly. Said daughter is now 42 years old.

Susan Cumber
Stoke-by-Clare, Suffolk

SIR — I was interested to read the report that Alice bands are returning to fashion. I wonder whether this has been accelerated by the increasing number of people who choose to wear their spectacles and sunglasses, even on dull days, on their heads.

Richard Baxter
Shelton, Staffordshire

SIR — I visit London infrequently, and normally dress in my "tidy London clothes". I am bewildered by at least half the people I come across being dressed as Michelin men (even in the very mild weather), and/or being wired up to various electronic devices.

Have the Martians finally arrived?

Mary von Westenholz
Ware, Hertfordshire

SIR — Around 4.15 this evening, in Sloane Square, I walked passed a Met policeman in uniform with his hands in his pockets, an open-neck shirt and no tie. Is this now the norm?

In despair,

Simon Davie
London SW1

SIR — I read with interest (in your review of Dan Jones's book on King John) the views of Richard of Devizes following a visit to London in the 12th century. Apparently it was full of "actors, jesters, smooth-skinned lads, Moors, flatterers, pretty boys, effeminates, singing and dancing girls, quacks, beggars and buffoons."

I visited London last week...

Johnny Cameron
Fyfield, Wiltshire

SIR — I have happily worn my red corduroy trousers throughout many, many winters. Indeed, when I give them a rest, friends often express disappointment at their absence as they cheer them up. Chums express the same opinion in the summer should I not be wearing my now very faded pink chinos.

I was wearing both colours long before the so-called "hipster" upstarts arrived and, God and my tailor willing, will still be wearing them long after their silly sartorial tastes have moved on.

Robert Warner
Ramsbury, Wiltshire

SIR — I wish to report a rare sighting: a youth wearing neither drainpipe trousers, nor sporting an apology for a beard. Presumably nobody has acquainted him with the age-old dictum that young people express their individuality by copying each other.

Tony Lawson
Langley, Berkshire

SIR — The interest in what parents wear to take children to school reminds me of a friend who, when going to pick up his teenage daughter from a party late at night, always wears his pyjamas.

Pulling up outside the party he attracts the attention of someone coming out and asks if they will go in and tell his daughter that he is waiting outside, adding the rider that if she doesn't come out, straight away, he will come in to collect her.

She appears like the cork out of a bottle.

Peter Smales
Swallowcliffe, Wiltshire

SIR – You report that vicars may be allowed to conduct services in tracksuits and hoodies.

Why not pyjamas and dressing gowns for that homely feel beloved of the school gate?

Or if the House of Bishops really want to wake up church congregations, it's got to be mankinis.

Doff Hughes
Wickham Market, Suffolk

SIR – Pleas to be allowed to wear hats in church remind me of a priest who once stalked up to the pulpit, took the microphone from the rather surprised younger priest and barked: "People are claiming it is cold in church. Well, it's hotter in hell."

The matter was closed (and so, finally, were the church doors).

Noeleen Murphy
London SE22

SIR – Your fashion article, "Trainers now suitable for work and play", reminds me of a response from a member of the Norfolk aristocracy when asked if he had any trainers.

"Yes," he replied. "One in Newmarket for the flat horses, two in Lambourn for the jumpers, and a local gel who keeps a couple of point to pointers for us."

Nicky Samengo-Turner
Gazeley, Suffolk

TRAILER TRASH

SIR – My grandmother used to tell me that litter is a measure of how you are brought up: the working classes leave their litter behind, the middle classes take their litter home with them and the upper classes pick up other people's litter.

Gilbert Dunlop
Great Offley, Hertfordshire

SIR – My original irritation at having to pay for supermarket bags has turned to great delight.

The looks from my poorer neighbours, "the Joneses", when my husband places our Waitrose bags for life in the dustbin are almost as funny as those from "the Greens", on the other side, who know that, because of the thicker bags, we are also able to hide all the things we no longer need to make the effort to recycle.

Alison (Hyacinth) Benham
Salford

SIR – I suspect I am not alone in now having two kitchen drawers filled with carrier bags that have been lovingly saved as if they were precious heirlooms. May I remind your readers, and my wife in particular, that the new law has only set their value at 5p, not £50.

Steve Baldock
Handcross, West Sussex

SIR – I refuse to use my Aldi or Lidl carrier bags in Waitrose – am I a snob?

Keith Davies
Telford, Shropshire

DIGITAL DISEASES

SIR – My wife's two-year-old grandson lives in Perth, Australia, and currently has conjunctivitis. I now have conjunctivitis. He is the only person I know who also has it. I can only conclude that I have caught it via FaceTime.

Garry Gibson
Jedburgh, Roxburghshire

SIR – I understand that there is a proposal to use lasers to highlight people using mobile phones in the theatre.
    I would like to suggest tasers as more appropriate.

Ian Watson
Warlingham, Surrey

SIR – Now I have seen everything: a horse rider ambling slowly up the road while texting on her phone.

R.S.
Langport, Somerset

SIR – I have developed a theory along the lines of Darwinian evolution. Another few thousand years down the road man will have developed a third eye half way between the crown of the head and the forehead. This will prevent bumping into things when texting with the head bowed.

> **D.A.**
> Broadstone, Dorset

SIR – Recently, my wife was struggling with her iPad and inadvertently activated Siri, who asked if help was needed.

My wife muttered under her breath, "Oh, b***** off."

Siri replied, rather reproachfully, "'Goodbye' would be more polite."

Clever things these machines.

(I am withholding my name for fear of marital retribution.)

> **P.B.**
> Kennington, Oxfordshire

SIR – Watching Google's AI AlphaGo programme defeating Lee Se-dol at the ancient Chinese board game of Go, I was reminded of the American comedian Emo Philips: "A computer once beat me at chess, but it was no match for me at kick boxing."

> **Keith Gilmour**
> Glasgow

SIR – Many years ago, when I worked in the nuclear and offshore industries, it was always cynically remarked that no product would be accepted by the client until the weight of the documentation was equal to that of the product itself.

I have just bought a digital voice recorder. The recorder weighs 66 grams; the instruction manual, which runs to over 250 pages, and which is written in no fewer than 31 languages, weighs over 160 grams.

Andrew McEwen
Poole, Dorset

SIR — My computer screen keeps going black. Have I inadvertently found the dark web?

Hugh Collins
Wool, Dorset

SIR — As someone with the misfortune to have bought a computer installed with Windows 10, may I suggest that if we are not already under a cyberattack, the aforementioned is as close to the real thing as we are likely to get.

John P. Hunter
Shaw, Wiltshire

VODAFONE TORTURERS

SIR — When trying to arrest General Noriega on drug-trafficking charges, the Americans used repetitive loud rock music, blasted through large speakers, to wear down his resolve and drive him mad.

I wonder why Vodafone seems intent on treating their customers in the same way as a Panamanian dictator.

Joel Kissin
London SW3

SIR – It is reported that TalkTalk has had a ransom demand after being the victims of data theft. How on earth did the culprits manage to get through to the company to speak to somebody in authority?

> **Philip Moger**
> East Preston, West Sussex

SIR – In view of the time it takes to connect to HMRC perhaps they should play Handel's *Messiah* in full.

> **Malcolm Johnson**
> Petersfield, Hampshire

SIR – I recently telephoned the pest control department of Guildford Borough Council. I listened to all five verses of *A Mouse Lived in a Windmill in Old Amsterdam*. I quite enjoyed it.

> **Auriel Rankmore**
> Ash, Surrey

SIR – Included in the medley of hold music when telephoning our local doctors' surgery is the theme music from *The Ladykillers*.

> **Mik Shaw**
> Goring-by-Sea, West Sussex

CHIEF KILLJOY OFFICER

SIR – Your report on the Chief Medical Officer's latest alcohol advice reminds me of one of George Gurdjieff's pithy sayings. There are, he said, only two types of doctor

on this planet: the first kind helps you to die; the other
prevents you from living.

Mark Ellison
Long Buckby, Northamptonshire

SIR — When I was a medical student I had a textbook called
Clinical Pharmacology. In its section about giving advice to
patients was a rhyme as follows:

My doctor's issued his decree
That too much wine is killing me.
And furthermore his ban he hurls
Against me touching naked girls.
How now, must I no longer share
My life, with beauties, dark and fair.
Doctor, Goodbye, my sails unfurled,
I'm off to join the other world.

Perhaps Professor Dame Sally Davies should take note.

Dr David Layfield
Farnsfield, Nottinghamshire

SIR — As the medical profession comes to look more and
more like the provisional wing of the Band of Hope, I
cannot help recalling how, in the high and far-off times
when I was a student, the medical students were the heaviest
drinkers of us all.

On second thoughts, that probably explains a lot.

Sue McNaughton
Eastergate, West Sussex

SIR — I am now told I can enjoy only 14 units of alcohol a week. That's fine; I just won't enjoy the rest.

Ros Mackay
Porthallow, Cornwall

SIR — Some years ago I was at a lecture when the question was asked: "Why is the limit for women 14 units but 21 for men?"

The professor replied: "The levels are based on the amount individuals admit to drinking, and women are better liars than men."

Dr Alan Prowse
Leatherhead, Surrey

SIR — If I am to keep up with the amount of alcohol consumed by the average woman in Newcastle upon Tyne, I shall have to increase my consumption considerably.

Brian D. Hamilton
Ponteland, Northumberland

SIR — Since retiring, my evening routine has been to relax with a pint of Guinness as I listen to *The Archers*. But, due to the fiendish antics of this terrible fellow Rob Titchener, I have had to switch to a double malt whisky every evening to keep me calm.

Ron Kirby
Dorchester, Dorset

SIR — My local pub has its own suggestions for Dry January: dry gin, dry white wine, dry martini, dry cider.

Sandy Pratt
Dormansland, Surrey

SIR — What evidence is there that in Islamic countries or societies, which ban alcohol, they are healthier than the rest of us?

Michael Bashford
Bournemouth, Dorset

SIR — Attitudes to alcohol consumption vary with geographical latitude. The Mediterranean countries love it; the Fins ban it; and the English argue about it endlessly.

Peter Tillotson
Valencia, Spain

SIR — My wife and I were so depressed by your headline, "Give up all drink or risk dementia" that we found ourselves forced to open a second bottle this evening.

Rod Cochrane
Wanstrow, Somerset

SIR — So now it's official: I really am drinking to forget.

I.F.
Co. Kerry

SIR — My mother had dementia, but never drank, smoked or had sex other than while praying for forgiveness.

She did, however, do the *Telegraph* crossword. Could that be the cause of her dementia?

K.P. Jones
Halesowen, West Midlands

OF MICE AND MEN

SIR – A drug which has been found to reverse the effects of Alzheimer's disease in mice is the latest in a long line of drugs (to treat everything from heart disease to cancer) which have been discovered to be effective in mice.

Unfortunately, these treatments often run into problems when scientists try to apply them to humans.

I am just wondering: since we can now cure mice of just about everything, is it now possible to rear an immortal mouse?

A.W.
Bristol

FIRST POWER WASHER OF SPRING

SIR – One of the first harbingers of spring used to be the sound of lawnmowers chugging into life. This now seems to have been superseded by the drone of power washers.

James Logan
Portstewart, Co Londonderry

SIR – Today I saw my first schoolboy vaping (I won't mention the school). Is this, like the first cuckoo in spring, a good sign?

Rodney Hedley
London SE5

WATER TABLES

SIR – The residents of Eglwyswrw in Pembrokeshire have had to endure 82 continuous days of rain. They should, however, be comforted that they do not live in Norway.

Local folklore relates the tale of a visiting American tourist, standing in the pouring rain, asking a nearby youth: "Does it ever stop raining in this country?"

The Norwegian boy replies: "I don't know. I'm only 12."

Craig Kennedy
Brookfield, Renfrewshire

SIR – My husband came back from one of his solitary walks on the fells, in poor weather. I asked if there had been any bad moments and he said yes, there had: he was afraid someone who was approaching him was going to say hello. But the danger passed.

Sarah Latimer
Melton, Suffolk

SIR – After bailing out my flooded vegetable garden for the third time, I was somewhat consoled to be reminded that volatile climates are not new.

In 1768 the naturalist Gilbert White wrote: "A wet season began about 9th of June, which lasted thro' haymaking, harvest and seed-time, and did infinite mischief to the country."

Vanessa Travers
Epsom, Surrey

SIR — When I fully retired two years ago, I had a vision of long leisurely lunches in the garden with a well-chilled glass or two of white. So far, due to our Lancashire weather, I have managed three cups of tea.

Steve Cartridge
Egerton, Lancashire

SOLIPSISTIC STORMS

SIR — Abigail, Barney, Clodagh, Desmond and now Eva — ever since we started naming storms they have caused record damage. They are obviously encouraged by all the attention they are getting.

Peter Turvey
Guildford, Surrey

SIR — My late father was called Desmond, my later mother-in-law Eva and now the next storm is Frank, the name of my late father-in-law. Are they trying to tell us something?

Sue Ward
London N20

SIR — Is there a list somewhere of all the silly storms yet to come? It would be helpful to know which names to avoid for future family births. I also hope my name does not figure on the list.

Jeffrey Pack
London W5

HEY, JUNIOR

SIR — After years of ridiculing my parents for being unable to call me by my given name until they had gone through my brothers' and the dogs' names first, I now find myself doing the same thing to my sons.

Is anyone able to explain why a parent cannot call a child by their correct name at the first attempt?

Chris Bands
Priors Dean, Hampshire

SIR — According to your report, it seems that very few babies nowadays are being called Nigel. I put this down to collective national grief after the sad demise of Nigel Pargetter, who fell off a roof to his death in *The Archers*.

Ian Coldicott
Norwich

SIR — Your article about the shortage of new Nigels should concentrate the minds of new parents. I recently suffered a heart attack and now attend rehabilitation exercises twice a week. Our group of 12, which I am told is fairly typical, contains three Michaels and only three women.

Michael Gale
Windlesham, Surrey

SIR — My mother always told me I was her second favourite child. Unfortunately, I was her only one.

David Parker
Rhayader, Powys

SIR – Reading Alice Smellie's column about how proud
she was of her name reminded me of a favourite story of
my father's. As a child he and his friends would find people
with the name Smellie in the telephone directory, phone
them up and when the phone was answered, shout: "What
are you going to do about it then?" – and then hang up.

Zanzie Griffin
Sheldon, Devon

SIR – Alice Smellie's article reminded me of my friend
Susan Crap. At least she didn't have to spell it.

Mark Solon
London N1

A ROOM OF MY OWN

SIR – My wife and I decided many years ago that one part
of a happy marriage was to agree how all shared spaces be
decorated, kept and used, but that each should have one
room entirely as their own space, free of spousal diktat, in
which to be themselves.

Hers is light, airy and feminine, while mine is dark
and lined with over 1,000 books on military history; the
remaining space is largely devoted to oddments of militaria.

My wife has christened it, rather charmingly I think, the
Bower. It stands for Boring Old So-and-So Room.

Victor Launert
Matlock Bath, Derbyshire

SIR – When our family lived in Japan we had a small room within our lounge with obscured glass walls. From time to time our young son was sent there to count to ten and reflect upon his bad behaviour.

Upon our return to the UK the removal men were very keen to know where – and indeed if – they could unpack the box marked "naughty room".

Michelle Bull
London SW19

SIR – My office-cum-study in the barn adjoining the house is known as "the kennel". The dog and I both love it – a place in which we can fart in peace.

T.G.-G.
Chagford, Devon

SIR – My niece was having the utility room refitted when the then Leader of the Labour Party was in the dock for having two kitchens. The resulting space is always referred to as the Miliband.

Chris Swindley
North Luffenham, Rutland

A YEAR IN
POLITICS

CULTURE CLUB

SIR — I note that John Whittingdale visited a lap-dancing club as part of his duties. I wonder if any of your readers can help me understand whether lap dancing is culture, media or sport.

Malcolm Woods
Southend on Sea, Essex

SIR — One wonders if the sex worker is receiving support and counselling after finding out that she was having a relationship with an MP.

Alex Orr
Edinburgh

FACING UP TO BOATY

SIR — My understanding is that it is acceptable to change the name of a boat providing you tell the boat why. I trust, therefore, that Jo Johnson, the Science Minister, will have the courage to face Boaty McBoatface and publicly explain why her democratically chosen name is to be ditched in favour of something selected by her self-serving political masters.

Phil Sampson
Leighton Buzzard, Bedfordshire

SIR — Can I suggest that Sir David Attenborough now changes his name to Boaty McBoatface, thereby forcing the science and technology select committee to name the boat correctly.

Greig Bannerman
Frant, East Sussex

SIR — As a citizen of the USA, and a descendent of a participant of the Battle of Bunker Hill (the winning side, mind you), I feel I must state my disappointment with your Parliament for disavowing the UK public's overwhelming vote. In my opinion this is a perfect example of what is wrong with a constitutional monarchy.

Until such time as your Parliament restores the fine name, Boaty McBoatface, I shall be forced to boycott all things British, including my Friday serving of fish and chips.

And before you start slinging Donald Trump jokes my way, please keep in mind that if he is elected, it will probably hurt you more than it will me.

D.W.
Chicago, Illinois

NO, YOU KHAN'T

SIR — If Donald Trump becomes President will the Mayor of London be allowed into the United States?

Bob Stebbings
Chorleywood, Hertfordshire

SIR — Now that we have a Muslim mayor of London can we not have a Catholic monarch?

> **P.S.**
> Jersey, Channel Islands

SIR — In Scotland a state-educated lesbian Conservative has just become the Leader of the Opposition. In London a state-educated Muslim socialist of Asian origin has just been elected Mayor of London. Will we soon need positive legislation to protect Old Etonian WASPs seeking public office?

> **Anthony Rodriguez**
> Staines upon Thames, Middlesex

WHAM HAM THANK YOU CAM

SIR — Here in our favourite local pub, where current affairs are always discussed with all the seriousness they deserve, tonight we have been wondering: at formal occasions in Mr Cameron's old Oxford College, is the convention still observed that you must pass the pork to the left?

> **Brus Watters**
> Sherborne, Dorset

SIR — I once heard the CEO of a major British company say that he was disinclined to give employment to graduates with first-class degrees from Oxbridge because such people have spent all their time at university studying, instead of experiencing the elements of student life that allow them to become rounded individuals.

The fact that our Prime Minister behaved like most other students makes him a far better leader than a goody-two-shoes.

John Franklin
London N1

SIR – I believed that British politics was corrupt until I read that all Lord Ashcroft got for the £8 million he gave to the Tories was the offer of a post as a junior whip.

Dr John Doherty
Stratford-upon-Avon, Warwickshire

DCTRS ON STRKE

SIR – I notice that all the placards being held by the striking junior doctors in the recent strike were either typed or stamped.

Is this because we would not understand their protest if we had to attempt to read their writing on the placards?

Malcolm Freeth
Bournemouth, Dorset

SIR – Jeremy Hunt's decision to enforce his changes to the NHS suggests that James Naughtie's slip was not inappropriate.

I dare you to publish this.

Mark Davies FRCS
Old Chalford, Oxfordshire

SIR — What's the difference between God and the Health Secretary, Jeremy Hunt? At least God knows he's not Jeremy Hunt.

Susanna Bailey
Eaton Hastings, Oxfordshire

SIR — As it is practically impossible to book an appointment fewer than four weeks in advance, a strike by doctors at our local surgery would pass almost unnoticed.

Dennis Graves
Crowborough, East Sussex

SIR — In the room of the Oxfordshire hotel where I am currently staying there is a guest information book which states: "Should you have need of a doctor we can make immediate arrangements for you to be seen."

Is this the answer to the GP appointment crisis: book into an hotel in Oxfordshire?

B.G.
Harrogate, North Yorkshire

SIR — In order to cut demand and queues at GP surgeries, they should review my local doctor's surgery in the Peak District in the 1970s. The waiting room, a thin, non-soundproofed room next to the consulting room, ensured that one never went to the GP for anything other than a sprained ankle.

Patrick Fuller
Upper Farringdon, Hampshire

SIR — My best chance to see an NHS doctor is to visit a picket line.

Roger Powell
Worcester

SIR — I think I would have more sympathy with the junior doctors if, on the television news reports, they did not look so happy and excited, rather like schoolchildren who have an unexpected day off.

John Pigott
Ringmer, East Sussex

SIR — My battle with my spellchecker continues. Today's diary entry was mistakenly recorded as: "I passed some stinking doctors and washed them well."

Ian Thompson
Darrington, West Yorkshire

SIR — I do not understand why the doctors' strike should be a cause for concern. I find that with Google and YouTube there is very little that I cannot diagnose and treat.

Graeme Hawkins
Cambridge, Gloucestershire

SIR — I was very sorry to discover that, in spite of a 24-hour doctors' strike, I was still forced to endure an hour of *Holby City* on the BBC this evening.

Gareth Temple
Kessingland, Suffolk

SIR — In the long-running television series *Neighbours* Dr Karl Kennedy is multi-disciplined with expertise in gynaecology, oncology, paediatrics and neurology. He is also permanently on call and available for home visits at the drop of a hat.

Perhaps the NHS has a lot to learn from our antipodean friends.

Michael Cattell
Mollington, Cheshire

CHE CORBYN

SIR — When as a callow youth I first grew a beard, people thought I was trying to look like Che Guevara. Later, with designer stubble becoming trendy, I was compared to Yasser Arafat. Now, greying and ageing, I am, to my chagrin, suddenly likened to Jeremy Corbyn. Time to shave it off, I think.

Charles Garth
Ampthill, Bedfordshire

SIR — I wonder why the more left-wing a male MP is, the less likely it is that his jacket will match his trousers.

S.G.
Waterlooville, Hampshire

SIR — I see that Jeremy Corbyn wore a tie at the Labour Party conference but showed his contempt for such a bourgeois appendage by leaving a gap at the top of the knot.

Brian Checkland
Thingwall, Wirral

SIR — With apologies to P.G. Wodehouse, if Jeremy Corbyn at the Labour conference in Brighton was not exactly dishevelled, he was far from being shevelled.

> **James Rothman**
> Balcombe, West Sussex

SIR — Doesn't Jeremy Corbyn break the old rule that you can either be unconventional, or dress unconventionally, but not both?

> **A.J.H. Latham**
> Reynoldston, Gower

SIR — Jeremy Corbyn's politics, while not acceptable to a lot of people, can be regarded as the cost of living in a democratic society.

However, his decision to wear socks with sandals is beyond the pale.

> **G. Johnson**
> Gateshead, Tyne and Wear

SIR — Softly spoken, seductive and hypnotic — Jeremy Corbyn reminds me of Kaa, the python in *The Jungle Book*.

> **Rosemary Moorhouse**
> Lydeard St. Lawrence, Somerset

SIR — You report that Jeremy Corbyn had a "fling" with Diane Abbott in the 1970s. I wonder who slept on the left.

> **Charles Foster**
> Chalfont St Peter, Buckinghamshire

SIR — What do Jeremy Corbyn and Boaty McBoatface have in common? They were both nominated for polls which they duly won by a substantial margin at which point those responsible (35 MPs and the BBC presenter) regretted their nominations.

The main difference between the two is that the Labour Party is stuck with Corbyn.

T.P.
Disley, Cheshire

SIR — As one of the undoubted minority of your readers who actually like the Labour leader, I am becoming concerned about what appears to be an outbreak among your centre-right commentators of *Splenetic Corbynitus*, a condition that raises the blood pressure to dangerous levels and may, I fear, trigger gastric ulcers. While their concern about the future electability of the Labour Party is touching, the constant and terrible worry must be taking its toll.

Jonathan Hill
Thornton-le-Dale, North Yorkshire

NUCLEAR PRETENCE

SIR — If we replace Trident we spend £20 billion. If we don't, we lose our deterrent. Why don't we just pretend we've replaced Trident? We'll save £20 billion and keep our deterrent.

Neville Landau
London SW19

SIR — Never mind whether we should or should not replace Trident, your picture of the cracked and dilapidated nuclear red trigger is deeply disturbing. Can I suggest we quickly replace that?

Fintan Walton
Oxford

SIR — On the subject of deterrence, I am forced to wonder if Mr Corbyn has unilaterally abandoned the use of a burglar alarm in his house.

Roger Whittingham
Dawlish, Devon

SIR — Seeing Jeremy Corbyn brandishing a pair of scissors at a "cutting the ribbon" ceremony made me wonder if that makes him better equipped than his army will be?

J.D.
Chipperfield, Hertfordshire

LETHAL WEAPONS

SIR — I read your article entitled, "Do women soldiers have a killer instinct?" with an understanding perhaps greater than most readers.

Having served as a nurse in military hospitals for over 30 years I was in constant contact with those delicate beings, namely the female nurses of the Queen Alexandra's Royal Army Nursing Corps.

Having trained with them on military exercises and played a few games of rugby against them, I can assure readers that they are well up to "going for the kill".

The only problem would be stopping them.

Alan S. Cubbin
Weasenham St Peter, Norfolk

SIR – I don't know what my wife would do to the enemy but she terrifies me.

Leon Paul
Oundle, Northamptonshire

SIR – How long before we call Women in Combat WomBats, I wonder?

Paul Fothergill
Paris, France

SIR – Only vaguely apropos the recent decision to allow women to serve in the Infantry, is anyone else a bit concerned that our senior army officers nowadays seem so wet? Generals used to be known for their bristling moustaches and peremptory, commanding manners; their modern counterparts appear to be mild, bespectacled men who speak in the mild, placatory tones of a modern bishop, and haven't got a proper military moustache between them.

Of course, we all welcome the general feminisation of everything, but shouldn't the battlefield be an exception?

Anthony Denny
Buckfastleigh, Devon

WAITING FOR CHILCOT

SIR –

To report on the war, Blair summoned Chil-a-cot:
"I want plenty of pages — please fill-a-lot."
But unless I'm mistaken,
From the time it has taken,
Chil-a-cot must have been ill-a-lot.

David Atkins
Lyminster, West Sussex

SIR – The Chilcot report delays have helped me understand the concept of deep time.

Mark Solon
London SW12

SIR – On July 7, the day after Mr Blair held his extraordinary press conference following the publication of the Chilcot Report, *The Daily Telegraph* Personal Column, wherein we can read a daily bible quote, carried the following: "There is a way that seems right to a person, but its end is the way to death" (Proverbs 14:12).

Was this message intentional or merely a telling coincidence?

Chris Kilpatrick
Brafferton, North Yorkshire

HEIR TO BLAIRMORE

SIR – Am I alone in finding it ironic that the family trust of David Cameron, our "heir to Blair" Prime Minister, is called Blairmore Holdings?

John Waine
Nuneaton, Warwickshire

SIR – David Cameron talks of "aggressive tax avoidance". Surely the desire to hang on to one's own property is intrinsically defensive?

John Hart
Chelmsford, Essex

SIR – Last year I bought a bottle of duty-free malt whisky at the airport. Am I morally repugnant?

Lucas Elkin
Haslingfield, Cambridgeshire

SIR – There is an interesting disparity in the media's treatment of David Cameron and John Whittingdale, both MPs who engaged in legal activities that they wisely decided to cease before taking high public office. Cameron caused a media frenzy, while Whittingdale received discreet media coverage.

Is this because few in the media circus understand even everyday financial products and yet fully understand even bizarre sexual activity?

Stephen Lovesey
Wantage, Oxfordshire

SIR – The fuss makes me wonder what the modern media would make of former MPs such as the notorious Thomas Benson, MP for Barnstaple in 1747 and Sheriff of Devon. He was supposed to transport convicts overseas, but delivered them to his island of Lundy off the North Devon coast, to help in his smuggling activities (chiefly tobacco).

He owed the Exchequer thousands of pounds in unpaid duties. Finally, he attempted an insurance fraud by scuttling his ship, but a drunken sailor revealed the truth. The master of the ship was caught and hanged, but Benson escaped to Portugal where he died in comfort. That was a real scandal.

Elizabeth Hammett
Barnstaple, Devon

SIR – It is not the fact that Mr Cameron has been slightly reticent in making a statement about his finances that disappoints me, so much as the fact he has failed to make any significant money from his investments. Clearly other heads of state are doing much better.

Martin Bastone
East Grinstead, West Sussex

SIR – There used to be something reassuringly predictable about political scandals: if it was a Conservative, then sex would be involved somewhere; if it was a Labour member, you could be pretty certain it would be about money.

We now find a Conservative prime minister embroiled in issues involving money. If Jeremy Corbyn ever discovers sex, we'll be really confused.

Graham Hoyle
Baildon, West Yorkshire

SIR — As an impecunious wage slave, the goings-on relating to the super-rich and the Panama Papers have been fascinating — despite the fact that they are taking place at a level far above the Poundland Papers world I inhabit.

I was therefore delighted to read your story about Jeremy Corbyn being fined for a late tax return. Now there's a man I can relate to.

Rob Reid
Skelmorlie, Ayrshire

SIR — It was a former Labour politician, Lord (Roy) Jenkins, who in 1986 provided a memorable definition of Inheritance Tax: "[It] is broadly speaking a voluntary levy paid by those who distrust their heirs more than they dislike the Inland Revenue."

T.B.
Swinbrook, Oxfordshire

I'M FEELING UNLUCKY

SIR — My eight-year-old granddaughter was sent Christmas gifts from her father (who is working in the USA and estranged from her mother), as well as some personal property she had left by mistake on her last visit. The total declared value was $200.

Instead of receiving the gifts, she was sent a letter from HMRC requiring £34 in tax before the gift would be released to her after Christmas.

Following an intervention by the MP, HMRC wrote to say that "rules are rules".

Yes, but not, it seems, if your name is Google.
Makes you proud to be British.

Bill Thompson
Frankby, Wirral

SIR – I always wanted to be successful and am now pleased
to realise that I have achieved this goal. I paid more tax than
Facebook last year.

Ed McGrath
Bookham, Surrey

DISENFRANCHISING STUDENTS

SIR – Their lack of historical perspective and the immaturity
demonstrated by the students campaigning against the Oriel
College statue of Cecil Rhodes suggests that, rather than
lowering the voting age to 16, the Government should put it
back to 21.

Michael Staples
Seaford, East Sussex

SIR – Now that Oriel College is preparing an ex cathedra
ruling on the character of Cecil Rhodes, might not their
learned dons save historians everywhere much toil involved
in analysing complex source material and the like by issuing
an exhaustive catalogue of historical figures, clearly divided
into columns of "Goodies" and "Baddies?

Nikolai Tolstoy
Southmoor, Berkshire

SIR — The process can continue with the London Underground: King's Cross offends republicans; Waterloo upsets those who believe a Napoleonic victory in 1815 would have deposed the regency, so Regent's Park must go too; Mansion House becomes Council House; Oxford Circus can be renamed Ntokozo Qwabe Circus after the great Oriel Rhodes' scholar who started the kerfuffle; and as for Cockfosters...

Charles Foster
Chalfont St Peter, Buckinghamshire

SIR — I was interested to read Allison Pearson's report that the JCR at my old Cambridge college, Christ's, was considering "non-binary" loos. Actually, Christ's has always been quite innovative in this department. When they installed the first college bath house in Cambridge towards the end of the nineteenth century, the other colleges expressed amazement at this unnecessary facility, as undergraduates were up for only eight weeks each term.

David Nicholls
Manningtree, Essex

SIR — As Oxford seeks to display more portraits of gay people, may I suggest that Cecil Rhodes might be a worthy choice.

Michael Rye
Enfield, Middlesex

BOTTLE OF BRITAIN

SIR – David Cameron says he will "battle hard for Britain through the night" at the EU renegotiations.

He should know that until Britain leaves the EU, this is not permitted under the European Working Time directive.

Beau Nidal
Brussels, Belgium

SIR – As Mr Cameron has accepted such reduced negotiation terms he appears not so much to have battled for Britain but bottled for it.

David Wilson
Cottingham, East Yorkshire

SIR – Never has so little been promised to so many by so few.

William Wilson
London SW11

SIR – Why is it that when a man goes shopping armed with a list of needs and wants, he inevitably comes home without most of them and, those he does manage to get, are a pale imitation of the important things with which he promised to fill his basket?

Evelyn Evans
Evercreech, Somerset

SIR — "We do not pretend, and never have pretended, that we got everything we wanted in these negotiations. But we did get big and significant improvements on the previous terms.

"We confidently believe that these better terms can give Britain a New Deal in Europe."

That wording appears on page two of the Government pamphlet I and other voters received immediately prior to the 1975 referendum.

Allan Kirtley
Cobham, Surrey

SIR — I had a "once in a lifetime" vote in the 1975 European Referendum and I'm still here. Should I consult my physician?

Alan Jones
Rossendale, Lancashire

PROJECT INSANITY

SIR — Samantha Cameron has said she will make David Cameron leave Downing Street before he is driven mad.

His assertion that, if we leave the EU, war will break out in Europe indicates she is too late.

David Saunders
Sidmouth, Devon

SIR — David Cameron says Brexit could mean war. Colonel Richard Kemp says a united EU army could mean war. Former equality chief, Trevor Phillips, says more migration could mean civil war.

As a *Telegraph* Crossword addict, when can we expect some coded messages?

Bill Danby
Skelton, North Yorkshire

SIR – We must be considerably more important than I had previously thought if, by leaving the EU, we will single-handedly be responsible for World War III, international genocide and aggravated global warming.

Now, that is punching way above one's weight.

John B. Hunter
Cheltenham, Gloucestershire

SIR – Mr Cameron says that the cost of a foreign holiday will rise by £230 if we vote to leave the EU. But who wants a foreign holiday during WWIII?

Steve Cattell
Hougham, Lincolnshire

SIR – I'm confused: is Mr Cameron's WWIII going to cause Mark Carney's recession or will the recession bring on the war?

Michael Ross
Hastings, East Sussex

SIR – It's a good job we are having a proper debate over the EU referendum – how else would the Prime Minister have discovered that Brexit might lead to war?

Only a year or so ago, David Cameron was of the view that, without significant reforms, he would be prepared to lead the Leave campaign. I dare say that, with further research, he will come to the conclusion that pestilence and famine would follow Brexit.

Alasdair Ogilvy
Stedham, West Sussex

SIR — The latest rumour is that if we leave the EU, my testicles will turn square and fester at the corners. Can anyone confirm if this is true?

Peter Walton
Buckingham

SIR — Should I be building a really, really big wooden boat, or am I too late?

Graham Whipp
Barnoldswick, Lancashire

SIR — It is an undisputable fact that if we vote for Brexit on June 23 the nights will start drawing in.

Mac Fearnehough
Holmesfield, Derbyshire

SIR — In his latest intemperate outburst David Cameron resembles King Lear in his revenge speech against his daughters: "I will do such things — what they are, yet I know not, but they shall be the terrors of the earth".

Perhaps, like Lear, Mr Cameron "is not in his perfect mind".

David Saunders
Sidmouth, Devon

SIR – Following David Cameron's dire warnings of the outcome of Brexit, I now await the opening of the Fourth Seal.

Sue Mawson
Gurnard, Isle of Wight

SIR – If all the dire predictions of the Remain campaign were to be realised, it seems likely that we would qualify to receive aid from overseas – perhaps even from the EU – so why worry?

Frank Felton
Stapleford, Cambridgeshire

SIR – I wonder what Mandy Rice-Davies would have said about the Chancellor's predictions of doom on Brexit?

T.B.
Dummer, Hampshire

SIR – How can anyone believe what George Osborne says when he is not wearing a yellow hard hat and hi-vis vest?

Garth Tomlinson
Hull

SIR – Half-witted footballers rip off their shirts whenever they score a goal. Could David Cameron tell us why he rips of his jacket whenever he wants people's support?

Brian Christley
Abergele, Conwy

SIR – I cannot imagine space travel safety would be immune from the evidently all-embracing dangers of a Brexit. How sensible therefore to bring Tim Peake back to earth ahead of the vote.

John Hellings
Emsworth, Hampshire

SIR – Yesterday I warned an elderly lady she was about to be run over by a bus. Should I apologise to her for scaremongering?

Paul Fulton
Wood Norton, Norfolk

I'M IN...

SIR – Hemmed in on all sides by lycra and V signs while driving on Sunday I was struck how similar Brexiteers and cyclists really are. Both groups have every right to pursue their cause, but in so doing they ignore the safety of not only themselves but others too.

Jeremy Raybould
Sanderstead, Surrey

SIR – Slowly but surely the average Englishman has come to an understanding of "smart casual", embracing chinos and linen jackets to great effect. I fear Brexit may put this at risk.

Sue McLellan
London SE26

SIR — While listening to Leave campaigners it occurred to me that the last time I had heard similar unsubstantiated promises of a rosy future was about 40 years ago when I was sold an Endowment Mortgage.

Paul Eastaugh
Hurst, Berkshire

SIR — Every time Nigel Farage's UKIP bus stops, it blares out the theme music from *The Great Escape* — an escape from the EU, I presume. Maybe he hasn't actually seen the film or perhaps his judgement is very poor, as the actual escape was an unmitigated disaster.

So keep on playing the music, Nigel — as a dire warning.

Richard Cook
Southampton

SIR — Nigel Farage, George Galloway and now Boris Johnson. The faceless bureaucrats of the European Commission are beginning to look positively attractive.

Mike Jones
London E4

SIR — Why are those employed by the British government to put its policies into effect always "civil servants", while those who do the same for the European Union are always "bureaucrats"? Surely their functions are essentially the same?

Piers Paul Read
London W12

SIR – Following Boris Johnson's odious comparison between the EU and Hitler, might it not be time to recreate the ancient Athenian system whereby once a year the people could vote to send an individual into exile for a good few years.

As a classicist, Mr Johnson would understand how the system worked.

William Stebbings
Gretton, Gloucestershire

SIR – Is a Hitler obsession compulsory for the London mayoralty?

Robert Dobson
Tenterden, Kent

SIR – Boris Johnson describes himself as a freedom fighter. Does this mean David Cameron will call him a terrorist?

Allan Reese
Forston, Dorset

SIR – A net contribution of £160 million a week seems a very fair price to put Michael Gove and Boris Johnson in their place.

Richard Gowland
Heacham, Norfolk

SIR – I am 77 and have voted Tory in every election since I qualified to vote, but God help this country if our future relationship with the EU lies with the *Daily Mail* and the old farts in the shires who run the local Tory constituency groups.

Grenville Peacock
Elstead, Surrey

SIR – This octogenarian voted wishing he was a four-armed oriental deity: one hand for his stick, one for the ballot paper, one for the pencil and one to hold his nose while he voted Remain.

David Eliot
Seavington, Somerset

SIR – If the EU would agree to swap one migrant for one English football fan I would vote for Remain.

Malcolm Allen
Berkhamsted, Hertfordshire

SIR – How do I stop my parrot repeating "take back control"?

Alan Sabatini
Bournemouth, Dorset

SIR – Following your front-page report that the majority of *Telegraph* subscribers favour Brexit and Boris for Tory leader, I am afraid that I shall have to ask for my daily copy to be delivered in a plain wrapper.

Brian Austin
Alfreton, Derbyshire

I'M OUT...

SIR — Large posters have started to appear in windows here reading "I'm in". Wishing to express my own referendum position, but minus street frontage, I found in Brighton last week a pink rosette stating "I'm out and proud".

I am surprised at the extraordinary reaction to this. Only the other day a cathedral verger gave me a knowing wink and a thumbs-up sign. I am amazed that UKIP have not made them more widely available.

David Johnson
Oxford

SIR — I have never thrown an egg at a politician — but I like the idea that one day I might.

In order to protest in this way you need to know who the responsible person is, where you can find them and where there is a good throwing position.

In the EU none of these requirements are satisfied. So I am voting out.

God Save the Queen.

Martin Callingham
London W1

SIR — "Name any MEP" was one of tonight's questions on *Pointless*. I couldn't.

Martin Moyes
Holt, Wiltshire

SIR – Britain's membership of the EU is like being married to Rob Titchener in *The Archers*: coercive control.

Geoffrey Whittington
Startley, Wiltshire

SIR – If anyone had taken a partner in 1973, married in 1975, and their spouse had taken their money, spent it on grandiose schemes and two homes whilst inviting more partners to join, would they still be together?

Mark Robbins
Bruton, Somerset

SIR – It would appear that letters on Brexit signed by numerous signatories are guaranteed to be published.

Rupert Godfrey – Husbands for Brexit

Julie Godfrey – Wives for Brexit

Yogi – German Shepherds for Brexit

Woodie – Cocker Spaniels for Brexit

Luther – Moggies for Brexit
Stert, Wiltshire

SIR – I note that the cost of leaving the EU will be £4,300 per household. Sounds fair. Can I pay ours now?

Martin Higham
Wimborne, Dorset

SIR — My grandson is being radicalised at school. He has been told by a teacher that to remain in Europe is the only option and that he should persuade his grandparents to vote accordingly in June.

Michael Meadowcroft
Durham

SIR — I have advised my wife that I am to vote Remain in the coming referendum. As she invariably adopts, on principle, the opposite stance to any political or ideological pronouncement of mine, I feel sure I have guaranteed at least two more votes for Brexit.

Pete Matthews
Winchester

SIR — Is not "ever-closer union" a precise definition of a black hole?

Alan Green
New Malden, Surrey

SIR — If our "leap in the dark" is as successful as that of Singapore when it left Malaysia I will be more than satisfied.

Brian Gilbert
Hampton, Middlesex

SIR — If President Obama is so keen on the EU perhaps he should join.

D.M. Jobson
Hindhead, Surrey

SIR — President Obama may like to reflect on the fact that America once "left" the largest and most powerful organisation in the world — the British Empire. As to how well they have done since is open to debate.

Adrian Waller
Woodsetts, South Yorkshire

SIR — At last, some clarity in the debate. Tony Blair is in favour of remaining and so I will vote to leave.

David Reed
Ticehurst, East Sussex

SIR — Surely another good reason to support Brexit is the hostility demonstrated by the French crowd to Andy Murray at the French Open.

Ros Heron
Leamington Spa, Warwickshire

SIR — Having trawled through my wardrobe, 90 per cent of it bought in M&S, I could find not one garment from the EU. Sri Lanka, China, the UAE, Cambodia, Turkey, India, Bangladesh and many more seem to be the major manufacturers.

This is a relief, as if we do leave the EU I know that I will not go naked.

Sandra Mitchell
London W13

SIR — I was all set to vote Leave, but the BBC's *Newsnight* and *Channel 4 News* have put me in a dilemma. Their scrupulously impartial reports from around the country would suggest that leaving is the preserve of life's "losers" — notably the less articulate who live on run-down, rain-spattered estates.

I'm now wondering if I'd be better off joining the Remainers who evidently have jobs and seem to enjoy better weather.

C. Hatton
Hay on Wye, Powys

SIR — I read the letters column avidly. After an in-depth analysis lasting all of ten minutes, I have come to the following conclusion: the people who are going to vote Remain are glass half empty types, while the Leavers are definitely glass half full.

David Nesbitt
Irthlingborough, Northamptonshire

SIR — A friend and I were discussing the bureaucratic complications he had to cope with during his one-year secondment in Brussels.

I inquired how many people worked in the EU offices there.

"Oh, about 10 per cent," he replied.

Jeremy Watson
Marnhull, Dorset

SIR – We have the ultimate authority on how to vote in the referendum. For millions of years Britain was part of the European land mass. About half a million years ago God, in his wisdom, created a glacial river which separated the two land masses. If the Almighty wanted us to join the EU would he have created that river?

Dr John A. Rees
Stratford upon Avon, West Midlands

SHAKE IT ALL ABOUT

SIR – The more arguments I hear about staying in or leaving the EU, the more I hear myself singing the words of the *Hokey Cokey*.

Janet Brown
Ulgham, Northumberland

SIR – In or Out? Why didn't we just ask Hawk-Eye?

Colin Henderson
Cranleigh, Surrey

SIR – Having changed my mind several times during the EU referendum debate, I now find myself forced to vote Remain as the terms and conditions of the three-year guarantee on my new cordless power drill purchased two weeks ago are limited to its use within the European Union.

J.W.
Cortsley, Wiltshire

SIR – Which way do I need to vote to get BBC iPlayer to work in a Europe "without barriers"? Currently it only works in the UK.

> **James Purves**
> Marden, Wiltshire

SIR – If we vote to leave the EU, will the BBC give us back Fahrenheit in the weather forecasts?

> **Paul Eward**
> Ross-on-Wye, Herefordshire

SIR – In principle I support Brexit. My overriding concern, however, is whether my 82-year-old husband will continue to receive a free ski pass in France.

> **Jane Cullinan**
> Padstow, Cornwall

SIR – When our local Waitrose car park is full, complete freedom of movement is not possible. We have to wait for entry: one in, one out. Why can this simple procedure not be adopted by the UK?

> **Simon Olley**
> Kemsing, Kent

SIR – I can't decide. If I vote out, can we have Marathon, Jif and Opal Fruits back?

> **Sheelagh Sizeland**
> Carterton, Oxfordshire

SIR – If we Brexit, how much wine will I be able to buy on a booze cruise?

Pam Laney
Burbage, Wiltshire

SIR – I have absolutely no idea whether the UK should stay in the EU. Can I give my vote to someone else? I was thinking of the Queen, as she doesn't have one.

Charles King
South Croydon, Greater London

SIR – It's not difficult to form a judgement here. Simply ask yourself how the characters in *Dad's Army* would have reacted in these circumstances and vote accordingly.

T. Williams
Sheffield

SIR – Is the word *Brexit* allowed in Scrabble? It doesn't appear in my dictionary.

G.A.
Wingrave, Buckinghamshire

SIR – *Brexit* sounds like a combination of a breakfast cereal and a laxative.

Alan Titchmarsh
Rushmere St Andrew, Suffolk

SIR – Faced with the prospect of 120 days of people banging on about whichever side they support my task is to decide which side is going to lose so that I can vote for them. Then I will be able to spend the next 25 years sitting smugly in the corner saying, "I told you so."

Howard Larkin
Hurst, Berkshire

SIR – As a 71 year old I doubt the referendum vote will have any major consequence on me during my remaining life span. Playing the Devil, the temptation is to vote "out" and watch how such a step into the unknown unfolds. It could provide an interesting period in my life.

Let's hope I resist the temptation.

G.T.
Yarm, North Yorkshire

SIR – Let me make this clear: I will be voting for the campaign which uses that phrase the least between now and June 23. I believe they will be the ones who actually are clearer on what to do next.

Peter Owen
Claygate, Surrey

SIR – When one liar calls another liar a liar which liar should we believe?

Barrie McKay
South Cerney, Gloucestershire

SIR — After all the hype, the only people to have gained from the referendum campaign are the punk band The Clash, whose record *Should I Stay or Should I Go?* has been played incessantly on Radio 4 for weeks.

Ken Tucker
Wotton under Edge, Gloucestershire

SIR — Everyone knows that nicer people vote Remain, and I want to be seen as nice.

However, it looks like Leave will win, and I don't want to be on The Wrong Side Of History.

I'm going to have to count celebrity endorsements to make a final decision.

Richard Lucas
Edinburgh

SIR — I would be more inclined to accept Richard Branson's endorsement of the EU if firstly, he lived in Europe and secondly, he were not trying to get to the moon.

Charlotte Joseph
Lawford, Essex

SIR — Perhaps the signatories of yesterday's letter from the luvvies could now turn their mighty minds to other topics of great import? I'd greatly value Cumberbatch, Emin and Nighy's views on interest rate levels, HS2 and identifying the true nature of dark matter.

Steve Baldock
Handcross, West Sussex

SIR — Are there any right-wing luvvies?

Peter Bolton
Oxford

SIR — Can we now expect to see a letter in the *Telegraph* signed by Shakespeare, Elgar, Constable, Wolfe et al telling us that they managed just fine outside the EU?

J.A.D.
Portland, Dorset

SIR — Has anyone else noticed the most pronounced difference between the referendum campaign and last year's general election? There has not been a sight or sound of Russell Brand anywhere.

Edward Thomas
Eastbourne, East Sussex

CRYSTAL BALLS

SIR — Having recently undertaken some lengthy motorway journeys my wife and I decided to conduct our own referendum poll. We took a tally of all British passenger cars that passed us, noting whether they displayed an EU or non-EU number plate.

Of 1,000 cars noted, 559 had the non-EU plate and 441 the EU one. So for our poll it was 55.9 vote Leave and 44.1 Remain.

Unscientific, I know, but probably as good as the polling organisations have been in the last few elections.

Stephen Whytock
Fleet, Hampshire

THE PAIGNTON TEA PARTY

SIR — This morning I came downstairs to find that we had voted to leave the EU, the Prime Minister was going to resign and that we had "got our country back".

I quickly made a pot of tea.

Mike Thompson
Paignton, Devon

SIR — How sad that we shall probably never learn whether Her Majesty was observed to purr this morning.

Clare Humm
Stamford, Lincolnshire

SIR — Well done to all fellow fruitcakes.

David G. Ford
Seaford, East Sussex

SIR — I am slightly discombobulated by your statement that the "less educated tended to back Brexit".

Dr Ian Hindle JP PhD MSc BDS FDSRCS FFDRCSI
Scopwick, Lincolnshire

SIR — Heard at 6am that Brexit had won the referendum. Have been waiting all day for sky to fall in.

Is it safe to go shopping?

Alan Gloak
Glastonbury, Somerset

SIR — Should we be sending our fleet of small boats
across the Channel to pick up our boys at the Euro 2016
Championship?

Stephen Wright
Pewsey, Wiltshire

SIR — The effects of Brexit seem to have kicked in rather
sooner than I had anticipated. I have just sent an email
enquiry to a French company requesting a quotation for
one of their products. The reply, by return, stated: "We do
not sell to the UK. Try the Brazil office."

Guy Frankham
Norwich

SIR — I was staying in a hotel in Germany's Black Forest the
day after the referendum vote and ordered a slice of the
famous local gateau.

"What is the filling?" I asked when it arrived.

"Pure cyanide," replied the manager with a broad smile.

Charles Owen
Carnforth, Lancashire

SIR — Will any German foreign minister understand that
Boris Johnson playing cricket after the Brexit vote was
absolutely the right thing to do?

Anne Jappie
Cheltenham, Gloucestershire

SIR — I wonder if my German-made washing machine and car are fitted with "defeat devices", programmed to stop working as soon as the detail of the UK exit is finalised.

Only time will tell.

John Smith
Great Moulton, Norfolk

SIR — Would anyone like to buy one of the "proper" toasters I've stockpiled?

Edward Buckley
Ramsey, Isle of Man

SIR — Every other country in the world would have had riots, tear gas, Molotov cocktails and tanks prowling the streets. That is not the British way of doing things. We quietly join an orderly queue; we smile nicely at the official handing us our polling card; then we use a pencil (nothing too sharp, mind you) to remove all the ruling elite from power.

What a thoroughly British way to have a revolution. No wonder so many foreigners want to move here to live.

Peter Bryson
Yorkshire

SIR — To coin a phrase by Speaker Bercow: The oiks have it. The oiks have it.

Robin Gardiner
Melksham, Wiltshire

SIR — Was the Brexit rebellion against the establishment part of a trend triggered by the high-handed rejection of "Boaty McBoatface"?

> **David Stanley**
> London SW6

SIR — What will *Telegraph* letter writers blame everything on now?

> **Bryan K. Conery**
> Whitehaven, Cumbria

SIR — May I suggest that we revert to pounds, shillings and pence. My grandmother gave me half a crown some 50 years ago. It remains in my piggy bank and I would like to cash it in.

> **Alistair Donald**
> Stirling

SIR — Now that the pound has fallen sharply against other currencies and we have, at a stroke, fallen from the fifth to sixth largest economy in the world, surely Project Fear should be renamed Project Understatement?

> **Stephen Coles**
> Wavendon, Buckinghamshire

SIR — Will we see crowds of migrants waiting in Kent to try to get into the EU?

> **Arnold Burston**
> Rolleston on Dove, Staffordshire

SIR — Would the last Polish plumber to leave the country please turn off the water.

> **Phil Mitzman**
> Ely, Cambridgeshire

SIR — I am standing at my front door awaiting delivery of the promised milk and honey. It has yet to arrive. Whom do I sue?

> **Andrew Keen**
> Stewkley, Bedfordshire

SIR — We appear to be moving from optimistic Brexit to pessimistic Brickingit.

> **Geoff Wilson**
> Radcliffe on Trent, Nottinghamshire

SIR — Earlier today I overheard one of our staff voicing his "deep concerns over Sterling". It soon became apparent that he was referring to the selection of Raheem Sterling, the England footballer.

Life goes on.

> **Anthony Perrin**
> Farnham, Surrey

SIR — The referendum result has at least solved one problem. Now we will not need a new runway at either Heathrow or Gatwick.

> **Peter le Feuvre**
> Funtington, West Sussex

SIR — It has all been a terrible mistake. We thought that we were voting to leave *Eurovision*.

Dr P.F. Hart
Harleston, Norfolk

SIR — One of our hymns today was *Dear Lord and Father of mankind / Forgive our foolish ways*.

Jonathan E. Godrich
Clee St Margaret, Shropshire

SIR — Who would care to join me in a new party I am forming called UKEP – the United Kingdom European Party? Its sole aim would be to campaign for the UK to rejoin the EU.

Dr Richard Marsh
Strathdon, Aberdeenshire

SIR — Perhaps when the new trading deal has been agreed with the European Union we could call it the "Common Market".

Richard Starks
Alnwick, Northumberland

SIR — As London prepares for the climax of Pride in London this weekend, I was amused to see a tight T-shirt pass me with the slogan: "Chill it bitch — Britain came out years ago".

Robert Gardener
London SW15

SIR — Nine people voted on what to do for dinner. Four chose to stay at home.

Of the five that wanted to go out, one wanted pizza, one wanted a kebab, one wanted Chinese, one wanted Indian and one misheard the question and now wants to stay home after all.

Why are we still going out?

M.F.
Utrecht, Netherlands (formerly of Birmingham)

SIR — Apropos the second referendum petition, is this what is known in political circles as the moaning after pill?

Huw Beynon
Llandeilo, Carmarthenshire

SIR — I would respectfully ask those Remainers still seeking to overturn the result to hurry up. If there is to be a civil war we need to get on with it and the days in which I might usefully die on a battlefield defending British democracy are, sadly, numbered.

Matthew Garrard
Southam, Gloucestershire

SIR — I was a firm Remain voter but now the deed is done I am doing my best to look for a positive way forward.

How good would it be if the British could rid themselves of the annoying habit of kissing both cheeks as a greeting? Let's regain our personal space; it might just help us all cope with the shambles we find ourselves in.

Pip Billington
Winchester

CHINS UP, DAVID

SIR – While David Cameron may have mixed feelings about recent political events, on the plus side at least he will be able to re-join White's, dust off his shotguns and get back into a morning coat for weddings.

Jeremy Nunn
Kimpton, Hampshire

SIR – Having listened to Mr Cameron's hum on the way back into Number 10 after his final press conference, I'm pretty sure it was the Rolling Stones hit from the 1960s: *It's All Over Now*.

Steve Thomas
Brackley, Northamptonshire

SIR – Whoever replaces Mr Cameron, will he please refrain from being photographed (a) tieless and (b) holding his wife's hand.

Alison Fenton
London W1

A DAY IS A LONG TIME IN POLITICS

SIR – Sadly, I am listening to *The Archers* much less frequently now. I find *The Every Day Story of British Politics* far more gripping.

Judy McRae
Walton-on-Thames, Surrey

SIR — I have started reading my *Daily Telegraph* from front to back, instead of the other way round.

Liz Wicken
Foxton, Cambridgeshire

SIR — Are there others of a certain age who feel that they are living in an episode of *Yes, Minister*? Is Sir Humphrey going to turn up and sort everything out?

Anne Knight
Brede, East Sussex

SIR — Surely now is the moment for the Queen to call upon Tom Hiddleston to form a government of National Unity?

Jonathan Higgins
Morden, Greater London

SIR — Watching the now regular resignations from Jeremy Corbyn's shadow cabinet is very much like watching an old-fashioned England middle-order batting collapse.

The difference is that normally the wickets don't fall until the other team has starting bowling.

Brian Gedalla
London N3

SIR — Momentum. Wasn't that the boy's team name in the second series of *The Apprentice*?

Tim Bochenski
Bramhall, Cheshire

SIR — Now that Nigel Farage has some spare time on his hands, might he consider opening a real ale bar in Brussels?

Located opposite the European Parliament (with a branch in Strasbourg, of course), "Les Deux Doigts" would be a fitting memorial to his political career.

Bob Ballingall
Farnsfield, Nottinghamshire

SIR — I expect to see a new version of Cluedo in the shops in time for Christmas — one where the characters are Conservative Brexit and leadership campaigners.

W.K. Wood
Bolton, Lancashire

SIR — Michael Gove may have denied, on five occasions, that he is equipped to be prime minister of the United Kingdom. However, we should remember that Saint Peter denied, on three occasions, that he was a Christian and he became the first Pope.

John B. Reid
Monkstow, Co Dublin, Ireland

SIR — Has no one told Michael Gove how *Macbeth* ends?

Sheelagh James
Lichfield, Staffordshire

SIR — The recent shenanigans by Michael Gove brings to mind the mixing of two proverbs by a friend: "I wouldn't trust him with a barge pole."

Keith Davies
Telford, Shropshire

SIR — What is the Latin (Boris may know the Greek too) for "I came, I saw, I bottled it"?

Richard Robinson
Letchworth Garden City, Hertfordshire

SIR — So was that Boxit?

Simon Tilling
Bildeston, Suffolk

SIR — Paul Weller of The Jam was remarkably prescient when in 1979 he wrote *Eton Rifles*: "What a catalyst you turned out to be: loaded the guns, then you run off home for your tea — left me standing like a guilty schoolboy."

Royston Deitch
London N5

SIR —
'Twas Brexit, and the slithy Gove
Did gyre and gamble all the way:
All mimsy was the Boris, Gove,
And the man's wrath helped May.

Chris Rogers
Loddiswell, Devon

MAY OF THE ROVERS

SIR — Much is being written about Theresa May's early life and how she intends to lead the country outside the European Union. But it is an indication of how guarded she is of her opinions that we have no idea which football team she pretends to support.

Mervyn Vallance
Maldon, Essex

SIR — I would like to wish Theresa May the best of luck in her new position. May I suggest that her first task should be to make sure that Mr Cameron has not left his daughter behind at Number 10.

R.B.
Tinahely, Co. Wicklow, Ireland

SIR — With all these state-school-educated women in the new Cabinet, will the whips ensure that there are some ex-public-school male MPs sitting in televisual shot behind Mrs May at Prime Minister's Questions in order to show diversity in the Conservative Party?

Michael Staples
Seaford, East Sussex

SIR — Let's hope Theresa May's husband Philip is not normally referred to by his initials, as it could cause confusion.

Tim Coles
Carlton, Bedfordshire

SIR — Some Germans apparently refer to Angela Merkel as *"unsere Mutti"* (our mum). How long before Brits (but presumably not Andrea Leadsom) start talking of Mother Theresa?

M.B.
Addis Ababa, Ethiopia

SIR – Boris Johnson? Foreign Secretary? And everyone said she had no sense of humour.

Please tell me someone was filming Mr Juncker when he found out.

S.P.
Birmingham

SIR – I note that Boris Johnson wrote a biography of Winston Churchill, perhaps seeking to draw parallels with his own political career.

May I suggest that, given recent events, his next subject might be The Grand Old Duke of York.

Gareth Corser
Bradfield St George, Suffolk

SIR – I am reading Charles Dickens' unfinished last novel, *The Mystery of Edwin Drood*, and I came across a passage describing the unintentionally droll Mr Grewgious, guardian to Rosa Bud. The description is a dead ringer for someone currently in public life:

"He had a scanty flat crop of hair, in colour and consistency like some very mangy yellow fur tippet; it was so unlike hair, that it must have been a wig, but for the stupendous improbability of anybody's voluntarily sporting such a head."

P.B.
Hampshire

SIR – I now have a female head of state, a female Prime Minister, a female Member of Parliament, a wife and two daughters, all of whom in some shape or form will influence what I do. I do not want to hear any more about lack of opportunities for women.

David Swanbrow
Sarisbury Green, Hampshire

SIR – When Margaret Thatcher was in power I was in San Diego. A taxi driver asked: "Geez, are you going to let a woman run things?"

I replied: "Every 500 years or so the men go rotten and we have to call the women in."

It seems that the time period is shortening.

Geoffrey Bishop
Malvern Wells, Worcestershire

SIR – Now that all the Leavers have Left and the Remainers Remain, all that remains is for the Remainers to finish off the leaving.

Tim Snelgar
Newbury, Berkshire

SIR – Now I am even more confused about the correct use of *may* and *might*.

Douglas Potter
Burnham-on-Crouch, Essex

THE USE AND
ABUSE OF
LANGUAGE

STRENUOUS ATTAINMENT TESTS

SIR – I considered myself highly literate. I am an Associate
Professor with a PhD who has published five poetry
collections, one novel and numerous scholarly articles. I
have been a professional journalist, a BBC TV producer and
Chair of the National Association of Writers in Education.
I have made a living out of reading and writing.

But I scored only three out of 10 on the sample SATs test
for 11 year olds.

Does that make me suddenly illiterate, or does it
suggest that linguistics is not literacy? Unless time is spent
cultivating a passion for reading instead of preparing
children for tests, we could end up with the most truly
illiterate generation this country has ever produced.

Dr Maggie Butt
London N14

SIR – It seems I have unknowingly been using subordinate
conjunctions all my life. Would I lose the use of my fingers
if I wasn't aware that they are dactyls?

Graeme Hawkins-Dady
Wolverhampton

SIR – Who needs the EU when a British government
department issues an edict about children's use of the
exclamation mark?

Bryan Haylock
Hadleigh, Suffolk

SIR – The Book of Revelation (New International Version) contains 55 sentences ending with an exclamation mark. Yet behold! Not a single one begins with what or how!

John Wallbridge
Wolverhampton

SIR – In 1862, Victor Hugo, eager to know how *Les Misérables* was selling, sent a telegram from the south of France to his publisher in Paris asking simply "?".

In arguably the most eloquent use of the exclamation mark, his publisher's reply was "!".

Nicholas Young
London W13

SIR – I have just heard a commentator on Sky Sports say "he played the hole lovely". I think this entirely justifies setting the SATs.

John Roberts
Wokingham, Berkshire

A QUESTION OF SPORT

SIR – Can I be the only person longing for a sports event winner to answer the interviewer's question "How do you feel?" with "With my fingers"?

Andrew Blake
Shalbourne, Wiltshire

SIR – During the recent one-day international against Pakistan, one of the commentators observed a player was "batting well with the bat".

I'm still trying to work out how he might manage without.

Leonard Glynn
Bristol

SIR – While listening to the *Test Match Special* coverage over the last few days I have come to the conclusion that Geoffrey Boycott's remuneration as a commentator must be based on the number of times he repeats himself.

Ian Franklin
Totnes, Devon

SIR – My thanks to Jim White for identifying the theme tune of the Champions League as being from *Zadok the Priest*. I always thought they were shouting: "Lasagne".

D. Keevil
Birmingham

FRUITY FIESTA

SIR – I have just bought a box of clementines from the supermarket. On the side of the box it says: "Celebrate Spanish Citrus".

Never having been asked to do this before, I seek advice from fellow readers on how to proceed. Should I arrange a street party? Or something more low key?

Anthony Tanney
Wickham Bishops, Essex

SIR — I recently bought some French cheese with bilingual packaging. In French it was described as being "pour sandwich", while in English it was "for baguettes".

Christopher Jolly
Chigwell, Essex

A CUNNING PLAN(ET)

SIR — The California Institute of Technology has discovered a ninth planet beyond Pluto. A spokesman described it as "the most planety planet of the solar system". That spokesman wouldn't be Professor Edmund Blackadder, would it?

Ian Looker
Dorchester, Dorset

QUEASY MEDIA

SIR — As few, if any, television or radio commentators can properly enunciate the phrase "quantitative easing", may I suggest "queasing".

John Maloney
Biggar, Lanarkshire

SIR — Can we have any confidence in the man in charge of HS2 when he does not even know how to pronounce the letter aitch?

Andrew H.N. Gray
Edinburgh

SIR — Could someone please tell the BBC not to say "one pence"? It makes me talk to the radio rather louder than I normally do.

Mark Lanyon
Chedworth, Gloucestershire

SIR — One can only rue the day when the received pronunciation of yesteryear was replaced by "imitated Pestonunciation" — a laconic drawl that places the emphasis on all the wrong syllables.

The latest disciples of the Robert Peston school of speech seem to be Laura Kuenssberg, following fast on the heels of Lucy Verasamy.

Bring back John Cole, say I.

David Denton
Belfast

SIR — A newspaper reviewer on Radio 4's *Broadcasting House* informed us that "IDS literally went for George Osborne's jugular" with regard to disabled benefit cuts.

It's such a pity that no photographer appears to have been there to record this extraordinary event.

David Brown
Lavenham, Suffolk

SIR — I believe there must be a table of adjectives available to journalists.

I suggest:

"Legend" — faded pop artist.

"Personality" — no known expertise.

"Star" — anyone on television with a speaking part.

"World-renowned" — expert in little-understood subject.
"Celebrity" — almost anyone else.
There must be others.

Ray Melvin
Bury St Edmunds, Suffolk

SIR — Why do so many journalists *utilise* a word with seven
letters when it would be just as effective and more efficient
to *use* one with only three?

John Stephenson
Andalucia, Spain

SIR — When did the word *bought* become *purchased*?

Dr P.E. Pears
Coleshill, Warwickshire

SIR — Why have television interviewers gone to such absurd
lengths to extend the simple salutation "Good morning"?

The greeting briefly became "Good Morning to you,"
and has now become "A very Good Morning to you".

The interviewee, not wishing to be outdone, then
responds with: "And a very Good Morning to you, too."

Nicholas Young
London W13

SIR — Again my ears are assailed by "forward planning"
(*Today* programme this morning). I am waiting eagerly for
someone to tell me about their "backward planning".

Brian Frater
Praze an Beeble, Cornwall

SIR – A few years ago in our local bookshop, a poster advertised the latest Harry Potter book which you could *pre-order*.

I told the lady behind the counter that I didn't want to pre-order it, I just wanted to order it. She said that wasn't possible.

Geoff Jones
Ross-on-Wye, Herefordshire

SIR – Could we not consign *uptick* to the dustbin? Apart from its inelegance surely the prefix "up" is superfluous? I have never seen a downtick.

Peter Lee
Waterloo, Merseyside

SIR – No wonder Lord Grantham's ulcer burst after hearing his daughter, Lady Edith, inform him that she was going to "meet up" with a friend in London. In the 1920s everyone was quite content just to meet.

C.A. Delahunty
London W2

SIR – Those in charge of the musical content of *Downton Abbey* should be congratulated for ensuring that the cast singing *Auld Lang Syne* in the final episode pronounced *syne* with a soft "s" and not, as is usual, with a hard "z".

It was a rare treat. Well done.

Lin Thomas
Aberfeldy, Perthshire

SIR — As a user of subtitles when watching television I was intrigued to see that an "Anti-war hole" exhibition has just opened at our local art gallery.

Owen Hay
Stanway, Essex

SIR — We often see subtitles on the screen for foreigners, even when they speak clear, intelligible English.

Please could we also have subtitles for many of the reports from British vox pops. All too often my wife and I turn to each other and ask: "What did he say?"

P.R.A. Barron
King's Worthy, Hampshire

SIR — My dearly beloved wife would appreciate it if you could somehow stop anyone on television saying "revert back" and "reverse back". She feels that my ranting at the television may be risky for the blood pressure.

I can still remember my old English professor explaining that "tautology means saying the same thing — not, I hasten to add, saying the same thing twice, as that in itself would be tautologous".

I hope to get out more in the better weather.

Tom Boyd-Smith
Norton-on-Tees, Co Durham

SIR — The weather forecasters regularly remind us to "wrap up warm". Where can I find this thing called warm in order to be able to wrap it up?

Barbara Bannister
North Frodingham, East Yorkshire

SIR – The temperature where I live has reached 23 degrees centigrade today. I am a bit worried because I don't think we were told by the weather forecasters that it was going to be quite so hot, and in particular we were not told to "drink plenty of fluids".

Michael Lavelle
Scaynes Hill, West Sussex

I AM VERY CROSS TODAY

SIR – Why is it that all nuisance calls always start with the caller, who is completely unknown to you, asking, "How are you today?"

Have they any idea how insincere they sound? Who trains these people?

Maurice Anslow
Malvern, Worcestershire

SIR – When I collected my coat from the cloakroom at the Barbican Centre last week, I was rather bemused when the young man handed it back to me with an "Enjoy!" But I have to say that, pan-fried later that evening, it was surprisingly tasty and tender.

C.H.
Newmarket, Suffolk

SIR – Why do we need to "fudge" an issue when fudge, especially Devon fudge, is so tasty and invigorating?

Hyder Ali Pirwany
Okehampton, Devon

SIR – As a very old man I envy young people their energy and verve but not their refusal to commit themselves wholly to any emotion. Is prefacing what they say with "I am like" simply an opt-out for the real thing?

Robert Vincent
Wildhern, Hampshire

SIR – A friend of mine who does not like being wished "The Peace of the Lord" during church services responds with "Your place or mine?" He assures me that this usually has the desired effect.

Derek Wellman
Lincoln

WEDDING NIGHT BLUES

SIR – I am getting married soon and was completing an email to the registrar outlining, amongst other things, the music we wish to have played during our ceremony.

My phone helpfully translated *Eine Kleine Nacht Musik* to *Wine Kleenex Nacho Music*. Doesn't that sound like the most tragic night in ever?

Jonathan Oliver
Reigate, Surrey

SIR – This morning our local church's forthcoming Notice Sheet had this wonderful offer: "The third Thursday drop-in is at Christ the King this week, 2 to 3.30 pm. Anyone who fancies a drink and a chap is welcome."

Penelope Money-Coutts
Peppard Common, Oxfordshire

GOODBYE AND GOD BLESS

SIR – A leading cinema chain has banned an advertisement containing the Lord's Prayer in case it offends those of other faiths or of no faith. Perhaps it should also ban all films containing the word "Goodbye" which is, after all, merely a contraction of "God be with you".

Nigel Peake
Emsworth, Hampshire

SIR – Might I suggest that cinemas ban all advertisements which imply that buying things makes one's life better? That oft-unnoticed belief-system is slowly ruining everything.

Adam Wasenczuk
Eastleigh, Hampshire

PC CRUSADERS

SIR – Instead of crying "Allahu Akbar", perhaps the Manchester Police should instruct the bomber in their next reconstruction to employ the old Crusader war cry:

THE USE AND ABUSE OF LANGUAGE

"Deus vult". It may lack modern verisimilitude but it should mollify the diversity lobby.

Julian Waters
Standford, Hampshire

SIR – Why hasn't Winnie-the-Pooh joined Titty from *Swallows and Amazons* as an unacceptable name?

John G. Prescott
Coulsdon, Surrey

SIR – Changing the name of Titty to Tatty is the worst of political correctness. As nouns and verbs are so often muddled today it is surprising that Roger, the ship's boy, wasn't also renamed.

Edward Church
Selling, Kent

THE LAST CUT IS THE DEEPEST

SIR – Of all the cuts our Police have had to endure of late the unkindest, and certainly the most irritating, has to be their reduction to a single syllable by Theresa May in her recent speech.

Peter Hoskins
Calverley, West Yorkshire

SIR – Does anyone think Nicola Sturgeon can string a sentence together without using the words *Tory* or *progressive*?

Alastair Cannon
Bridport, Dorset

SIR — With regards to Cameron's "working mothers", could a pair of "stay-at-home mothers" care for each other's children (for equal pay) and thus become "working mothers"?

B. Sanders
Brighton

SIR — A "reformed EU" is now more important than "hard-working families" to MPs. A new vote requires a new mantra.

Maurice Hastings
Bickington, Devon

SIR — It was interesting to read that Lord Rose is "delighted to join the In Campaign's board as chair". I wonder who will sit on him first.

R.B.
Lincoln

THANKS, DAVE

SIR — The drafters of those circular emails which are sent out from time to time by Mr Cameron and Mr Fallon should be told that the only thing that irritates one more than being addressed by one's Christian name by someone one does not know personally is to find it inserted, for emphasis I presume, again in the body of the text.

David Vaudrey
Doynton, South Gloucestershire

SIR — Recently I had to make a complaint to a public service after my emails had been ignored. Yesterday I received a reply telling me that someone had been told to respond to me "without haste".

Does no one read what they have written before sending it any more or are they simply being honest?

Dr H.J. Williams
Prestatyn, Denbighshire

TAKEN TO TASK

SIR — A friend of mine has received a letter from one of his employees proffering his resignation. His stated reason for leaving was that the job was "too task orientated". Can your readers suggest what he means?

C.W.
Aughton, Lancashire

SIR — I was surprised when ringing the office from a payphone in 1985 to hear a colleague say: "I'm so busy I haven't got time to swing a cat." A few years later the firm's young telephonist told me that she recognised a new male client because she had "a feeling of rendezvous".

Gregory Moore
Bledlow, Buckinghamshire

SIR — People who mix their metaphors make my goat boil.

David Shaw
Codford St Mary, Wiltshire

SIR — An acquaintance of mine who worked for HMRC said that he had examined a tax return for a sex worker who described her occupation as a "contractor for the demolition of temporary erections".

Vincent Shanahan
Watford, Hertfordshire

REIGN IN THE SUBS

SIR — I read in my *Telegraph* TV guide on Saturday that Chris Evans has "reigned in" his shouting; and in the magazine that Stella Tennant has taken over the design "reigns".

Have your journalists been spending too much time covering Her Majesty's birthday?

D.N.
Westgate on Sea, Kent

SIR — I was alarmed by the caption accompanying the photograph on your Letters page today: "Fox hunting in Wales".

Surely: "Exercising hounds in Wales"?

Chris Bands
Priors Dean, Hampshire

SIR — In your report on the Government's EU leaflet you say that the Government is spending "taxpayers' money" on its production. As the Government has no money of its own, all its spending is raised from taxation. Whether it spends "money", "taxpayers' money" or even "hard-working taxpayers' money" appears to depend on the degree of effrontery felt by the reporter.

G.G.
Leominster, Herefordshire

SIR — I suggest that the Government should employ a proof-reader for its Universal Jobmatch site. When applying for cleaning vacancies I am often asked for my experiences in hovering, moping and weeping.

Stefan Badham
Portsmouth

SIR – Local papers are often a source of amusement. This week ours carried a photograph of a happy couple celebrating a "reprisal" of their wedding vows. One wonders if "renewal" might have been a better choice of word, unless of course they had *Fight the Good Fight* sung at their wedding.

Nora Jackson
Uttoxeter, Staffordshire

SIR – Congratulations to Allison Pearson for the *Telegraph's* first "from whence"of the year. The target (to beat?) is 44 from 2014, or 27 from 2015 – mostly from the Sport category.

Richard Weeks
Felixstowe, Suffolk

SIR – I'm puzzled when your reports replace missing words with a row of dots.

Recent quotes read:

"You've had your 10 minutes, you f...... b......... I'll f...... knock you out."

I guess that the missing words are as follows:

"You've had your 10 minutes, you frightful bounder. I'll finally knock you out."

Could this form the basis of a party game?

Desmond Clark
London SE2

SPLIT INVECTIVES

SIR — I was amused to read the correspondence, from 1964, about split infinitives. I recall one of my schooldays from around that time when a friend and I were walking across a quad from the main school to the classrooms.

My friend looked to the heavens and declared, in a very loud voice: "Damn! It's going to bloody pee!"

He had not noticed our housemaster walking towards us. He stopped to tell my friend: "For heaven's sake, boy, please don't split your infinitives" — and went on his way.

Paul Cheater
Litton Cheney, Dorset

UNFASHIONABLE PUNCTUATION

SIR — I read with horror your report stating that the full stop is going out of fashion due to impatient instant messengers. When I send a text to my daughter, I use commas, semicolons, full stops and the rest. It grieves me when in reply I receive "Ta" and a happy face.

Malcolm Debonnaire
Reading, Berkshire

SIR — Never has anything been more important to one's future well-being than the hyphen.

I quote the difference between extra marital-sex and extra-marital sex.

Jim Wilkinson
Great Coates, Lincolnshire

SIR — A year or so ago I encountered the word "miniseries" in the entertainment section of a newspaper. I didn't know what it meant. Something to do with religion maybe? I recently discovered where to put the hyphen.

David Daborn
Weybridge, Surrey

SIR — An otherwise brilliant *Star Wars* was ruined in the opening moments when the phrase (and I'm not making this up) "In a galaxy far, far away...." scrolled out on to the screen.

I resisted the temptation to grab my granddaughter by the arm, abandon our various popcorn, Kia-ora drinks and nacho treats, and storm out of the cinema.

Imagine! Thousands of trillions of dollars spent on this long-awaited instalment and they don't even care that an ellipsis has three dots, not four.

Peter Anderson
Kettering, Northamptonshire

TREXIT
SIR — On the back of Brexit, might it be possible to reclaim our traditional pronunciation? Half the population seems to adopt the American pronunciation of *schedule* and *harassment* (the film *Fatal Attraction* has a lot to answer for).

John Ley-Morgan
Weston-super-Mare, Somerset

SIR — Why has the perfectly good English word *outstanding* been replaced by the ugly Americanism *stand-out*?

Graham Jones
Tytherington, Cheshire

SIR — Why do we now call riding "horse riding"? What on earth else would we be riding in this country? A camel?
I presume we are copying America, as ever.

P.G.
Winburg, Norfolk

CLOSET CLOSETS

SIR — My late grandmother would not say *toilet*, *loo*, *WC* or similar. She always referred to it as the *howsyoumawhatsit* and other bizarre constructions. We suggested she call it the sitting room, but she demurred.

Anne Jappie
Cheltenham, Gloucestershire

SIR — After many attempts to teach a girlfriend's daughter to use the word *loo* rather than *toilet*, we came to a compromise: *loolet*.

S.C.
East Molesey, Surrey

SIR — Your correspondent is quite right when she says that pronouncing your own name eccentrically isn't always snobbery. It is sometimes a matter of necessity. Back in the early years of the last century my grandmother knew a family whose name was Cockshit, which they pronounced "Coeshey".

> **C.A.**
> London SE22

WHEYFUL PUNS

SIR — Three cheers to Clearfleau for building a power station that runs on waste cheese — definitely the whey to go.

> **Godfrey Pratt**
> Old Buckenham, Norfolk

SIR — I have sympathy for the ticket collectors complaining of repetitive strain disorder. I recall a similar problem when a woman working for an international news agency brought the same problem to the attention of the press. I think she was suffering from Reuters cramp.

> **Jerry Dixon**
> Hythe, Kent

SIR — "100,000 operations face the axe during doctors' strike". I recommend that patients ask for a postponement until the strike is over and the scalpel returns.

> **Jim W. Barrack**
> Beaconsfield, Buckinghamshire

SIR — Andy Murray says that "having a baby makes it easier to unwind". Most of us just blame the dog.

> **Tim Barnsley**
> London SW16

SIR – Am I the only person who was convinced that Andy Murray's daughter would be called Annette?

Ros Fitton
Solihull, West Midlands

SIR –Tracey Emin has married a rock. Does this mean we shall soon be hearing the patter of tiny pebbles?

Wendy May
Hereford

SIR – My mother used to bake scones which were as hard as rock cakes. I would ask: "May I have a scone of stone please?"

William Neil
Caversham, Berkshire

SIR – I drove into Leominster yesterday and thought there must be a Dutch firm opening premises on the outskirts of the town. Then I realised it said "Snack Van Open".

Bob Best
Weobley, Herefordshire

SIR – "Men's brains wired to choose sex over food", you report. I can see this causing problems in restaurants.

Peter Baines
Sale, Cheshire.

SIR — Having read your report about the proposed strike by gravediggers in Naples, I have to wonder if this action will cause a spate of panic dying.

> **Vic Storey**
> Dereham, Norfolk

SIR — Men are advised today that carrying a mobile phone in their trousers risks their virility.

Verdi realised this some 150 years ago when he advised: "La donna è mobile". I gave our mobile to my wife.

> **Tony Pay**
> Bridge of Cally, Perthshire

SIR — In a fit of exasperation with her non-functioning email, my 79-year-old mother declared: "Well, I hope Heaven is analogue."

I've regrettably had to inform her that it's cloud-based.

> **David Lavelle**
> Coneythorpe, North Yorkshire

SIR — Nice to see the Rolling Stones formally making an exhibition of themselves.

> **David E. Owen**
> Eldwick, West Yorkshire

SIR — With voters shifting towards an EU exit, does that mean we have now entered a "winter of discontinent"?

> **Scott Charleston**
> Dunfermline, Fife

SIR — I fear that the referendum will result in the Untied Kingdom.

Charles Cocking
South Pool, Devon

SIR — Has the time not come for the EU to replace its anthem, *Ode to Joy*, with *Owed to Germany*?

Philip Wilson-Sharp
Fordwich, Kent

SIR — If Finland had an EU referendum would their Out Campaign be called Fixit?

Bruce Chalmers
Goring by Sea, West Sussex

SIR — Is there a better name for a person who hops from one highly paid job to another in the public sector than *quango-roo*?

Harry Ellis
Glasbury on Wye, Herefordshire

SIR — Surely the closing concert of the new BBC Proms series to be launched in Australia should be called the *Last Night of the Poms*?

Dennis Waterman
Ashburton, Devon

SIR – My thanks to the Australian Police for confirming that the discovery of £500 million worth of drugs hidden in bra inserts was indeed one of Australia's biggest drug busts.

Dr Alan R. Brace
Holcombe, Devon

SIR – With degree-level entry a minimum requirement, will police constables be too posh to cosh?

Jane Thomson
Godalming, Surrey

SIR – Congratulations to Major Tim Peake on winning the *Great British Take Off*.

Rodney Chadburn
Tattingstone, Suffolk

SIR – Because of the smoking at work regulations do the astronauts at the ISS have to go outside for a fag?

John Elliott
Broughton Astley, Leicestershire

SIR – Could a group of people smoking e-cigarettes be described as a nest of vapers?

Derry Gibb
Epping, Essex

SIR – Please don't get rid of 1p and 2p coins. I recently visited England and filled my pockets with such unwanted coinage. I found the change did me good.

Dr John Doherty
Vienna, Austria

SIR – On today's interview with Andrew Marr, George Osborne began every reply with "Well..." – even though he often did not answer the question. Does he think that where there's a well there's a way?

Frank Hill
Malvern, Worcestershire

SIR – Should we regard the Labour leader's closest adherents as being Corbyn copies?

W.I. Hooke
Rugby

SIR – The subtitles for the forthcoming ITV series on Shakespeare inform us that we shall be anticipating it with "baited breath". Sounds fishy to me.

Robert Vincent
Wildhern, Hampshire

SIR – I have heard that the next Mary Berry spin-off will look at fortified wine on a ship from Northern Ireland to the Republic of Ireland: *The Mary Berry Derry to Kerry Sherry Ferry*.

David Evans
Lymington, Hampshire

SIR – Your television review of the final episode of *War and Peace* worries that "Sunday nights won't be the same".

Don't panic. The BBC is already planning a retro series featuring vegetables cooked by Nigella in an especially low-cut empire dress: *Phwoar and Peas*.

Allan Reese
Forston, Dorset

BOX GOGGLERS

DOWNTON DIRECTIONS DEMISE

SIR – I have not seen a single second of *Downton Abbey*, but the demise of the series will be hard to bear. It has served as a useful reference point when describing where I live to American colleagues who assume all of us over here live in London.

"Do you know *Downton Abbey*? Well, I live near to that house, surrounded by that beautiful countryside…er, no, I don't have a butler."

Charles Thomas
Overton, Hampshire

SIR – Despite the Grantham household endlessly devouring the best culinary fare that Mrs Patmore and her basement buddies have served from 1912 to 1925, it seems that no one has ever done any washing-up. Each week, while my wife keenly follows the plot, I sit keenly waiting for someone to stand over a steaming sink or grab a tea towel. Actually, I don't think they've even got a sink.

Come to that, I've never seen anyone get up from the table, pull an apologetic face, and say: "Sorry, just got to pop to the old, you know…"

Robert Cox
Bough Beech, Kent

SIR – Which will be forgotten first? *Downton Abbey* or Jeremy Corbyn?

Joe Cole
Wanstrow, Somerset

SIR — Now that *Downton* has come to an end the charity shops can expect the return of their collection of sleeveless nylon nightdresses. It was always obvious that no one living in a pre-central-heating building with wide corridors and draughty windows would have wandered around in anything so skimpy.

Sue Doughty
Twyford, Berkshire

SIR — I fear we never watched *Downton Abbey* since we saw a trailer in which the senior couple (whoever they may be) were shown in a double bed. This display of proletarian sleeping habits was an anachronism. My mother attributed the fecundity of the poor entirely to the dearth of bed-rooms — an issue not considered in the conditions for the bedroom tax.

We have pursued an active married life for some 60 years without the need for sharing a sleeping place.

Many of the regrettable incidents in *Downton Abbey*, of which we have heard rumours, should surely be put down to mistaking a bedroom for a bordello.

Quentin de la Bedoyere
London SW19

SIR — Television dramas seem to suggest that the room in which one entertains guests is called the bedroom.

Professor Mark Hill QC
London EC4

POLDARK'S PECS

SIR — Having spent much of my life at boarding school, in the Royal Navy and in rugby changing rooms, I have seen tens of thousands of men with their shirts off but never one who looked remotely like the Poldark chap. This, presumably, is because they had better things to do than spend two hours a day in gymnasiums for cosmetic purposes.

Iain Gordon
Barnstaple, Devon

PEACE AT LAST

SIR — Hooray for the BBC. At last I know the ending to *War and Peace*.

L. Lines
Wadebridge, Cornwall

SIR — Am I the only person to be amazed that Pierre managed to keep his glasses on throughout his visit to the battlefield of Borodino?

Hubert Pragnell
Canterbury, Kent

SIR — The letter concerning the great length of *War and Peace* reminded me of how grateful I was for this when travelling in rural Afghanistan in the 1970s (something one could barely contemplate today).

Having been laid low with an attack of dysentery, the only available source of lavatory paper was my copy of *War and*

Peace. Reading rapidly, its nearly 1,500 pages proved to be just enough. Thank you, Tolstoy.

> **Keith Bradford**
> Penn, Buckinghamshire

SIR – I made short work of *War and Peace* whilst breastfeeding a voracious newborn throughout the night.

The only skill required was the deft juggling of a tiny baby with an enormous paperback.

> **Adrianne Alun-Jones**
> Stratford-upon-Avon, Warwickshire

SIR – Woody Allen can help those of your readers who find *War and Peace* a monumental struggle. Allen said: "I speed-read it. It's about some Russians."

> **Andy Palmer**
> Mappowder, Dorset

SIR – It is worrying to learn that when he wrote *War and Peace* Tolstoy forgot to include incest and other spicy titbits. We are indebted to BBC producers for putting right his omissions.

Agatha Christie was also very remiss in not anticipating twenty-first-century mores when she forgot to alter the N-word in her original title, which was recently changed by the BBC to *And Then There Were None*. Happily, the BBC was able to divert attention from her mistake by several injections of the F-word which she had also forgotten.

> **P.A.**
> Somerton, Somerset

SIR — Once again the BBC failed to do justice to Tolstoy in the final episode of *War and Peace*. Where, pray, was the lengthy second epilogue setting out the author's critique of historiography and philosophy? "Dumbing down" strikes once more.

John Oxley
London E15

PESTON BREAK

SIR — I am deeply saddened that Robert Peston has deviated to ITV. Where now is the incentive to do the washing up? His presence on the BBC's *Six O'Clock News* ensured a swift exit to the kitchen.

Jeff Palmer
Durham

SIR — First in the firing line were the tie-less Greek politicians; then Evan Davis on *Newsnight*; then Jeremy Corbyn for his sartorial inelegance; now Robert Peston, whose "relaxed" dress sense is under scrutiny.

Isn't it time that male politicians and journalists were judged, like their female counterparts, on what they think and say, rather than on how they dress?

After all, they are more than just pretty faces.

Dr Steven Field
Wokingham, Berkshire

TV TANTRUMS

SIR – It is interesting to read that Louise Minchin has complained to the BBC that her co-presenter Dan Walker is sitting in the best seat. My son and daughter used to argue endlessly over the very same thing – but they were three and five at the time.

> **Alan Elliott**
> Sudbury, Suffolk

SIR – With left-wing bias burnt into the DNA of the BBC it is hardly surprising that the presenters are fighting over who should sit in the furthest left seat on the sofa.

> **Martin Armstrong**
> Tunbridge Wells, Kent

SIR – A gentleman should always have the lady to his left. How else might he wield his sword in her defence or even raise his hat with his right hand unencumbered?

> **J.C.D. Patterson**
> Manningtree, Essex

SIR – Why doesn't Louise Minchin sit on Dan Walker's lap on the favoured side with a cat on the other end for balance? This would give a whole new slant to the programme and certainly increase ratings.

> **Chris Ebeling**
> Hundson, Hertfordshire

SIR — Surely the problem with male/female presenters could easily be solved by ridding us of the "old" gentlemen presenters — who wants to watch John Humphrys and the like when all I have to do is look across my sitting room?

Eileen Fawdry
Hampton Hill, Middlesex

MARITAL CHALLENGE

SIR — It is annoying that Jeremy Paxman never gives the answer to the final question on *University Challenge* after the bell has gone as it is invariably the only question I get right, thereby beating my husband who doesn't get any right.

Not that we are competitive at all.

Christine Brown
Richmond, Surrey

UNANSWERED QUESTION TIME

SIR — Waiting in Outpatients to see a Doctor, I fell into conversation with the attendant nurse about the previous evening's television.

"I was on *Question Time* once," she volunteered. "I was in the audience, right on the front row."

"Gosh," I replied. "That must have been interesting. Who was on the panel?"

"I can't remember," she said. "But David Dimbleby smells wonderful."

Sue Ajax-Lewis
Rustington, West Sussex

GOODBYE, MASTER CHIPS

SIR – Why, in the increasingly pretentious concoctions served up as meals on *MasterChef*, are there never any chips?

Here up North, no dinner worth eating is without chips, mashed or roasted spuds.

Brendan Palmer
Nottingham

STOP MENTIONING THE WAR

SIR – After an eight-week stint in the UK I have some news for the television-watching population: World War II is over. It finished 70 years ago.

Nick Lawther
Sydney, Australia

BEST ACTOR IN AN AWKWARD ROLE

SIR – Should not all the Oscar nominees be given an award for managing to look so delighted when the trophy goes to someone else?

John Anderson
Sidmouth, Devon

CHELSEA FACE SHOW

SIR – Once more the BBC is to be congratulated on its coverage of the Chelsea Face Show.

We were treated to a programme full of faces, many of which we had never seen before.

These faces spoke to one another at length, and some were presented with certificates for designing things apparently known as gardens.

From time to time this fascinating parade of faces was interrupted by a brief view, often at a very strange angle, of — my goodness — flowers. Fortunately, whenever this error occurred it was soon remedied by a swift return to another face.

Next year can the BBC please show some sense and let us see what the Chelsea Flower Show is really about. They can always make a separate programme about faces.

Rachel Hart
Stalmine, Lancashire

HOW MANY OAPS IS CHRIS EVANS WORTH?

SIR — Instead of giving the jaw-dropping salaries the BBC pays their celebrities in pounds, why not give it in the number of license-fee payers it takes to satisfy this folly? For example: Chris Evans (11,000 pensioners), Graham Norton (8,935 pensioners), Claudia Winkleman (3,600 pensioners) and Mary Berry (3,400 pensioners).

Brian Christley
Abergele, Conwy

SIR — Can anyone explain what criteria the BBC has in place for selecting the celebrities in *Celebrity Mastermind*? Certainly it seems that the simple facts of being widely known and able to answer straightforward questions aren't part of the process, so I wondered what the alternative route for selection might be.

Steven Broomfield
Fair Oak, Hampshire

SIR — May I suggest *Daily Telegraph* columnists and readers give up the BBC for Lent. Come Easter, they might experience the revelation of just how good the world's best broadcaster is.

Peter Langworth
London NW1

STUIPD BOYS

SIR — The new *Top Gear* without Clarkson, May and Hammond is rather like *Dad's Army* without Captain Mainwaring, Sergeant Wilson and Corporal Jones.

T.G.
Rainow, Cheshire

SIR — Surely the ideal team of presenters for the next series of *Top Gear* would be Nigel Farage, Boris Johnson and Prince Harry?

Simon Shneerson
Chorleywood, Hertfordshire

SIR – An acronym of Jeremy Clarkson's new programme, *The Grand Tour*, could be read as *Top Gear Two* or even *Three Geriatric Teenagers*.

Cameron Morice
Woodley, Berkshire

OFF-PEAK TRAVEL

SIR – While his rail journey programmes are edifying, well-presented and of not inconsiderable interest, can anyone explain why the majority, if not all, the trains used by Michael Portillo are entirely bereft of passengers?

Maurice Palfrey
Devizes, Wiltshire

TRAVELLING
HOPEFULLY

TICKET TO HIDE

SIR — Travelling out of Waterloo to Southampton on South West Trains recently the guard asked if all passengers could help him stop a cat boarding at New Milton — apparently the station cat tries to board and go for rides.

As the guard wandered down to check my ticket I asked for the cat's name. Straight faced, the guard replied: "I'm afraid I don't know that, sir, but I know he hasn't got a ticket. Good day, sir."

Everyone smiled and said nothing.

I love being British.

Paul Troughton
Southampton

SIR — Travelling home from London yesterday the train was once again half an hour late. Ironically my bedtime reading told me that of the 4,278 trains used by the French army to mobilise two million men in 1914, only 19 suffered the same problem. Perhaps they might still be able to teach us a thing or two?

George Watson
Woodbridge, Suffolk

SIR — May I quote from my *Baedeker's Great Britain*, written in 1890?

"The carriages of the more important companies are generally clean and comfortable, but those of the lines to the south of London leave much to be desired."

Plus ça change.

Terry Burke
Canterbury

WALLS OF THE ROSES

SIR — So the Chancellor will enable a tunnel to be built under the Pennines, linking Lancashire and Yorkshire. What all Yorkshiremen need to know now is: which side will the Customs and Passport Control be on?

Paul Harrison (Migrant Yorkshireman)
Terling, Essex

EMBARRASSMENT ON BOARD

SIR — May I make a heartfelt plea to pregnant ladies to wear "Baby on Board" badges? I have a horrible feeling that this morning my insistence on surrendering my seat may have caused considerable embarrassment.

Julian Waters
Standford, Hampshire

SIR — In the 1970s, when my father and I used to travel to work together on the notorious Dartford Loop Line into Charing Cross, we always had to stand for the whole journey. My father solved this problem by physically lifting out of his seat, by the collar of his school blazer, any young schoolboy he deemed to be occupying a seat which a woman or an older person should have been using.

Word obviously got around because after a while, the boys of a particular school would give up their seats the moment my father got on to the train.

Needless to say, I was highly embarrassed and used to try to stand as far away from my father as possible. Nowadays, of course, it would be deemed to be assault.

Jill Smith
Stalbridge, Dorset

SIR — I don't give up my seat for the blind.

Twenty years ago a blind woman entered my Tube carriage. She had dark glasses, a white stick, a dog — the full kit. I naturally offered her my seat, only to be berated: "I may be blind but there's nothing wrong with my legs."

She continued to make remarks the whole journey, much to my embarrassment and the sniggering amusement of fellow commuters behind their papers.

Eventually I reached my stop and sprinted off, only to realise when I got to work that I had left my briefcase behind. On calling London Underground I was informed that a suspect briefcase had indeed been found, the District Line suspended and the Bomb Squad called to Bow Road.

Upon eventually arriving at Bow Road by taxi ("It'll take a while, Guv'nor, Mile End Road's chocker. Bomb at Bow Road.") I was immediately marched to the station manager ("Yes, that's my briefcase. Yes, that's right, the one with *The Lover's Guide* video in it.").

Humiliation over? Oh no. Upon getting the crowded Tube back to the City, a ticket inspector got on. Naturally I hadn't bought a ticket when being marched down to see the station manager at Bow Road. I then had to explain in front of everyone why I was travelling without a ticket.

I can still vividly recall the face of the woman who screamed: "I'm late for an interview because of you."

Now I don't even like people in sunglasses.

H.A.
Hambledon, Surrey

TIN-POT ECONOMY

SIR – If the UK is really the fifth biggest economy in the world, can someone please explain why our roads are so ravaged by potholes?

Godfrey Brown
Tolleshunt D'Arcy, Essex

SIR – My local illuminated dot-matrix road sign currently reads: "Is your vehicle ready for winter?"

I feel that I should stand next to it with a placard reading: "Yes, but your roads aren't."

Jonathan Yardley
Wolverhampton

SIR – I welcome the lighter mornings. It is so much easier to spot the potholes on my journey to work.

Philip Jordan
East Malling, Kent

SIR – Can I suggest that chewing gum is spat into potholes in the road?

Steve Cattell
Hougham, Lincolnshire

SIR — The roads in Northamptonshire are some of the best looked after by the Highways Authority. Whenever there are potholes, they send a man or two out in a vehicle with a large can of spray paint. This is used to mark a careful rectangle around the pothole.

After several months the paint wears off and the Highways people send another man (or two) with a new can of spray paint.

Oh yes, we motorists are well looked after in Northamptonshire.

David J. Hartshorn
Badby, Northamptonshire

THE NEED FOR SPEED

SIR — You report a crackdown on speeding by Police Scotland. It was Bedfordshire Police who stopped me as I drove in a 30mph zone and said: "Nobody keeps to the limit on this road, sir, and as it's 11pm on Friday night, by driving at 29mph you're showing unusual behaviour. So, if you wouldn't mind getting out of the car..."

Alan Parr
Tring, Hertfordshire

SIR — "Police Scotland: we're ready for terror attack" — only if the terrorists are speeding on the way to their target.

Andrew Bell
Kirriemuir, Angus

SIR — A strong Scottish accent can be advantageous. Some years ago, while on holiday in Cape Cod, my brother-in-law, who hails from Shetland, was stopped for speeding.

The police officer spent at least five minutes attempting to take down his name and address before admitting defeat and wishing us a happy holiday.

Kirsty Blunt
Sedgeford, Norfolk

SIR — Our police say that they are so busy and understaffed that they can only attend to "vulnerable" victims. How is it then that, if I drive past a speed camera at slightly above the speed limit, in perfectly safe conditions, the same police force will find enough manpower to pursue me, prosecute me, endorse my licence and/or lecture me for a day on how naughty I have been?

E.M.
Hathersage, Derbyshire

SIR — Why do all speed limits on our roads end with a zero (20, 30, 40 etc.)? Such a lack of flexibility and imagination by those who wish to control us.

Bruce Pearson
Godalming, Surrey

MULTI-PURPOSE VEHICLES

SIR – Why does the latest generation of car models have to look so aggressive? They seem all to be snarling and about to take a bite.

> **Pat Rand**
> Settle, North Yorkshire

SIR – I am thinking of placing a sticker in the back of my car that states: "No baby on board, but I would appreciate it if you do not crash into me."

> **R.K. Hodge**
> Chichester, West Sussex

OCULAR KNOWLEDGE

SIR – Your article about London taxi drivers made me think of an incident which took place in the 1960s. A black cab, turning out from a side street near Trafalgar Square, clipped the wing mirror of a car. The irate driver jumped out of the car and shouted at the cabbie: "What's the matter with your eyes, man?"

The cabbie replied: "What you mean? I hit ya, didn't I?"

> **Tore Fauske**
> Woodmancote, Gloucestershire

SIR – Your article states that Transport for London have sought assurances from Uber on "important issues around strangers travelling together" with regards to UberPool, the new cab-sharing service.

I have been travelling with strangers for years on the Jubilee line, and I am none the worse, apart from an occasional assault on the olfactory senses.

Paddy O. Connor
London NW2

SIR — I have taken a black cab from Euston station on my last three visits to the capital. The first cabbie faked a breakdown as he didn't wish to go south of the river. The second feigned surprise that a road near the station had been closed, resulting in a big detour (the road had been closed for weeks). The third berated me for having the temerity to proffer a ten-pound note as he didn't have any change.

Uber, on the other hand, is fast, efficient and relatively inexpensive. If we don't embrace change we will stand still as a society.

Michael Cattell
Mollington, Cheshire

CAIRO, AFRICA

SIR — At Heathrow Terminal 5 I asked at a British Airways Information Desk which lounge I should use for a flight to Cairo.

"Is Cairo in Europe?" asked the man.

One hopes that BA provides atlases in the cockpit.

A.W.
Cairo, Egypt (not in Europe)

SIR — As an interesting example of passenger profiling, upon our recent arrival in India I had to assist a blind man in a wheelchair with providing fingerprints of both hands, including his thumbs.

Meanwhile, elsewhere in the arrivals hall, my youthful looking wife was ungallantly advised that her fingerprints were not required as she was "too old to be a terrorist".

Peter Forrest
London N6

THE PEOPLE'S BICYCLE

SIR — I am unimpressed by the exhibition of new-found environmental concern by car owners who feel aggrieved that their German cars' computers have been skilfully programmed to always indicate that emissions standards are being met.

Like most drivers, as long as my vehicle passes the MOT, I don't care what emerges from the exhaust pipe. If I gave a fig about the environment, I'd have bought a bicycle.

John Eoin Douglas
Edinburgh

SIR — Having delighted their customers with the Beetle and the Rabbit perhaps VW might consider naming their next sleek new model the Cheetah.

Chris Wood
Graffham, West Sussex

SIR – A small orange light appeared on my German-made electric shaver this morning. I think it indicates that I should buy a new shaver head.

Should I believe it?

David Leech
Balcombe, West Sussex

SIR – So now we know: when a product is marked "Made in Germany" it's not a boast, it's a warning.

Griff Griffith
London E11

LESSONS IN LYCRA

SIR – One day I used my walking stick to point out to a cyclist a no-cycling sign (which is routinely ignored). The cyclist took his flamboyant revenge by waving his arms and shouting loudly: "That old woman is threatening me with her stick."

On another occasion I spoke to another young male cyclist and, as he stared uncomprehendingly at me, it occurred to me that he might be a foreigner. I asked if he understood English.

To my astonishment, his reply was, "Madam, I *teach* it."

Anne Everest-Phillips
Sidmouth, Devon

SIR — Dartmoor ponies are to be painted with glow-in-the-dark stripes to prevent motorists from hitting them at night. Should these stripes also be applied to the many cyclists who ride around in dark clothes at night, without lights?

Ted Shorter
Hildenborough, Kent

SIR — Walking in the countryside this autumn I have noticed a significant increase in the number of cyclists I encounter. I have also noticed that those cyclists who wear Lycra are reluctant to speak, make eye contact or to adopt a pleasant face. I am left wondering whether this stems from a desire to be unfriendly, or is it as a result of their too-tight clothing somehow preventing their facial muscles from working?

Tony Collingswood
Stockbridge, Hampshire

SIR — The cyclists that amuse me are the "let's dress up and play Bradley Wiggins brigade", who cycle furiously up and down public footpaths and seafronts in full regalia.

It is akin to my dressing up as a Formula One driver to drive down to the local supermarket.

Neil Webster
Fulwood, Lancashire

SIR — Further to recent correspondence about Lycra louts, I cannot have been alone in noticing a group of these people cycling nine abreast up the middle of a major thoroughfare in a capital city, holding up the traffic, no hands on the handlebars — and all compounded by drinking alcohol as they did so.

Surely this sort of behaviour cannot be condoned? Or should it be?

A true Force de Tour. Well done, Chris Froome.

John Prime
Havant, Hampshire

SPORTING
TRIUMPH AND
DISASTER

THE GENTLEMEN'S GAME

SIR — I hope calls to ban tackling in schools' rugby are ignored. I sustained a nasty fracture dislocation of my ankle aged 17 in a school game. This lead me to my current profession as an orthopaedic surgeon specialising in foot and ankle disorders.

Even with a bad injury rugby gave me much more than it took away.

Michael Dunning
Battle, East Sussex

SIR — Like many of your correspondents I, too, was taught on the school rugby field that "the bigger they come, the harder they fall". As I have matured, however, I have come to the conclusion that a lot of brave men have been very badly hurt because they were silly enough to believe this.

John Todd
Stoke-on-Trent, Staffordshire

SIR — In my son's experience of junior rugby it's not the tackling you should be worried about; it's the biting.

Kevin Platt
Walsall, West Midlands

SIR — I played rugby at school, in the Army, at various clubs, and at various levels, until my forties.

I did not suffer any broken bones, concussion, or other severe injury of any description.

Throughout this time, I also played cricket. I suffered two broken fingers, a badly torn muscle and a broken nose.

Is the medical profession studying the wrong game, or was I just terrible at both?

Kenneth McKinnon
Bangor, Co. Down

NORTHERN ROOTS

SIR – The England cricket team walked off the field for lunch with "Rooooot" ringing in their ears as Joe Root approached his 200 against Pakistan.

BBC lunchtime television news covered sport with news about the Sunderland football manager, the Anniversary Games and the sailing, finishing with, "And that's all the sports news".

Is it because the England team contains too many Northerners?

Nicholas Nelson
Wimborne, Dorset

THE MEN IN THE WHITE SUITS

SIR – Watching Chelsea vs Tottenham Hotspur on television last night, I was appalled at the behaviour of the teams. The amount of tugging at an opponent's shirt left me feeling that something must be done. I was reminded of *The Man in the White Suit*, in which Alec Guinness played a scientist who discovered a material that was so strong when dry that an oxyacetylene cutter had to be used on it to make his suit. Sadly, it fell apart when wet.

If footballers had shirts that came away when excessive

force was applied to them, it might make a player think twice before tugging at an opponent. Otherwise we would end up with both teams topless.

Robert Ward
Loughborough, Leicestershire

SIR – At the end of a game of men's international football they exchange their shirts with the opposition. Alas this is not the case with women's international football. I'm sure it would encourage a greater following.

Brian Moy
Rochford, Essex

WORLD BEATERS

SIR – Would it not be a good thing to have a World Hooligan Championship, in which national teams of highly trained drunken louts compete to beat one another up? Not only would it be a popular spectacle among those who like that sort of thing, it would also take the pressure off football. Even better, Britain might win.

Nicholas Guitard
Poundstock, Cornwall

ENGLAND OUT OF EUROPE

SIR – Was losing 2-1 to Iceland really such a terrible result for English football? We could have lost by a huge margin if we had played Sainsbury's or Tesco.

Leonard Clark
Bristol

SIR – Did the England football team take this Brexit a little too seriously?

David Hewitt
Chelmsford, Essex

SIR – It is a sad reflection that today, as we remember the soldiers who fought for our country in the Battle of the Somme, our England footballers are pictured lying down, crying, because they lost a football match. They were too distraught to congratulate the winning team.

A.H.
Yate, Gloucestershire

SIR – I was walking my standard poodle in the fields today. As so often, he raced back to me at high speed and stopped dead about an inch from my left kneecap. He then did a quick turn, leapt over a nearby grass tussock and sped off at right angles.

In short, he has fantastic positional skill, he is incredibly quick-footed and he could be exactly what the England football team needs to end its woes.

A year's supply of dried tripe and a less-than-obscene fee could clinch the deal.

W.H.
Fishlake, South Yorkshire

SIR – Isn't it time that only players from the Championship and below were picked to play for England? It worked for Wales.

G.W. Doggrell
Kingsley, Hampshire

SIR – Having lived on a border town all my life where the Welsh were always fervent rugby supporters, it now seems very strange to me to have all my Welsh friends talking about football and all my English friends talking about rugby.

Doug Morris
Monmouth

WINNING POMS

SIR – I couldn't help but laugh out loud at the front-page headline in Australia's *Sunday Mail* following the England rugby team's 3-0 thrashing of Australia in the recent series: "Well done England. Now a second continent hates you as well".

Robert Readman
Bournemouth, Dorset

TOWEL BOYS

SIR – Given that the BBC's *Today at Wimbledon* is reverting to its traditional name and format I hope that Wimbledon's ball-boys and ball-girls will revert to their traditional role of collecting stray tennis balls, rather than acting as part-time clothes horses and personal valets for the players.

They should adopt the same approach as my daughter when presented with a used towel and simply drop it on the floor.

J.B.
Aldeburgh, Suffolk

SIR — A ladies' singles match, particularly in the first week at Wimbledon, lasts just long enough for corporate guests to drink a bottle of champagne with a bowl of strawberries before returning for the next men's singles.

Alasdair Ogilvy
Stedham, West Sussex

SIR — Why, oh why, when we could have been watching Roger Federer changing his shirt, did the camera pan instead to a football manager sitting in the stands?

Jane Cullinan
Padstow, Cornwall

SIR — This afternoon I thoroughly enjoyed a programme on BBC Two with John Inverdale, Jim Courier and Tim Henman sharing fascinating facts about tennis. It was, however, most inconsiderate of the BBC to try and distract their audience with an accompaniment of a tennis match between James Ward and Novak Djokovic.

Ian McIlwraith
Gosport, Hampshire

SIR — At social functions it has long been a dilemma to know how — without spilling one's glass — one is supposed give a round of applause to those making the speeches. This year, the Wimbledon crowd beneath the balcony appeared able only to whoop rather than clap respectfully, apparently for fear of disrupting their smartphone footage.

Is there a solution?

Jane Park-Weir
Ellisfield, Hampshire

SIR — If I can buy a seat for next year's Wimbledon, I want the one immediately behind Ivan Lendl's. The only time he stood up was the Championship winner from Andy Murray.

Allan Littlemore
Sandbach, Cheshire

MURRAY'S A CHICKEN DINNER

SIR — Congratulations to Andy Murray on another Wimbledon triumph. Is it not time that an "Andy Murray" is recognised as the official rhyming slang for curry?

J. Alan Smith
Epping, Essex

SIR — It is indeed time to rename Henman Hill. Perhaps Murray Munro in recognition of Andy's roots?

Tessa Fassnidge
Silverton, Devon

SIR — Outside the Wimbledon Championships, why is it that Andy Murray always looks like the kid at school who forgot his kit and had to get dressed out of the lost property box?

John Price
Meir Heath, Staffordshire

SIR — Judging by the photographs on your front pages today, playing tennis causes Andy Murray great anguish. He is fit, young and rich; why doesn't he do something he enjoys?

Sam Kelly
Dobcross, Lancashire

COURIR DE FRANCE

SIR — Chris Froome had the misfortune to crash his bicycle at one point during the Tour de France but continued on foot to complete that leg of the race. So is the bicycle in a cycle race an optional extra?

In the event of Lewis Hamilton bumping into the barriers at Monaco, may we expect to see him sprinting along the main thoroughfare to the finishing line like Usain Bolt?

Peter Thompson
Sutton, Surrey

SIR — Watching the crowds cheering on the Tour de France certainly gives the lie to the myth that French women don't get fat.

Sandra Hancock
Dawlish, Devon

SIR — You show a fine photograph that perfectly encapsulates the glitz of the Monaco Grand Prix: a nonchalant, glamorous blonde and a red Ferrari Formula One car.

I must, however, take issue with your caption which describes the "ear-splitting whine" of the cars. Today's hybrid machines discharge a muffled thrum so dull as to make my lawn mower sound sexy in comparison.

Zog Ziegler
Haw Bridge, Gloucestershire

A BRIDGE TOO FAR

SIR — With regard to the ongoing discussions as to whether the card game bridge is a game or a sport, if you have to change your shoes, it's a sport. I have yet to meet anyone who changes their shoes to play bridge.

Tim Sugg
Hope Valley, Derbyshire

SIR — Is bridge a sport? No, it is an obsession.

Julia Bishop
Leybourne, Kent

SIR — I've had a sports injury for years: a stiff neck as a result of playing too much bridge.

B.O.
Princes Risborough, Buckinghamshire

SIR — It seems entirely reasonable that bridge should be classified as a sport. After all, many top players appear to have mastered cheating already.

Philip Brennan
Oxhill, Warwickshire

TEN-MINUTE MILE

SIR — Thank goodness that widespread doping in athletics has been revealed. Now my records will be rewarded: one mile in 10 minutes and a high jump of three feet.

J.E. Barley
Hessle, East Yorkshire

SIR – When sporting prowess becomes a political objective the ends usually justify the means.

I raced in the World Rowing Veteran Championships in Holland in 1996. When the Dutch announced an age check on all competitors in this age-related event the Russian team immediately went home without comment.

J.A. Whitmore
York

SIR – I may be missing something but I am not sure how drugs could have improved the performance of the Russian curling team.

Helen Wynne-Griffith
London W8

SIR – All it needs for the world of sport to send a decisive message that cheating is impermissible is for every contender at Rio to deliberately throw their event, enabling the Russians to secure a pointless "triumph".

Enough to make President Putin take polonium in his tea?

Iain Colquhoun
Killay, Swansea

SIR – Considering his erratic behaviour over the past few years, might it not be a good idea to test Vladimir Putin for drugs?

Mark Rennie
Newcastle upon Tyne

HOME
THOUGHTS ON
ABROAD

GREAT EASTERN FACE-OFF

SIR — Having read about yet more amazing sporting achievements by President Putin I can hardly wait for his final showdown with an all-sports challenge to Kim Jong-un of North Korea. This will make even bigger news than the *Great British Bake Off* final.

> **K.T.**
> Rayleigh, Essex

SIR — We have given an unnecessary boost to Putin's ego by choosing a man that looks like him to play James Bond. As well as having a strong facial resemblance, Daniel Craig also likes to show off his muscles in a Putin-esque way.

> **Liz Wheeldon**
> Seaton, Devon

SIR — On reading the headline, "Perfume inspired by Vladimir Putin goes on sale in Moscow", I can only assume that it would be "Eau Sauvage".

> **Michael J.B. Watson**
> London SW18

SIR — With regards to Litvinenko, one has to admit that the Russians have made great progress in their chosen area of expertise. They no longer use the ice-pick.

> **M.V.**
> Great Missenden, Buckinghamshire

SIR – I am less concerned about the reasons Mr Putin has begun withdrawing his forces from Syria than about where he might be considering deploying them next.

Air Commodore Michael Allisstone (retd)
Sidlesham, West Sussex

SIR – When you consider how much trouble there was in Kyrgyzstan, including a mini-riot when a Briton thought their local sausage was horse penis, is it surprising that there is so much warfare in that part of the world?

Andrew J. Rixon
Hertford

WHILE THE EURO BURNS

SIR – I have just returned from a holiday in Greece. This may not be an accurate barometer of Greek economic health, but the men have stopped fiddling with worry beads. They are now fiddling with their mobile phones.

Philip Saunders
Bungay, Suffolk

ORLA GUERIN TRAVEL ADVICE

SIR – I am currently living on the continent for a few months for work. While observing the security advice of our Foreign Office, specifically about Brussels and Paris, I prefer to observe my own security barometer: the Orla Guerin index.

If I discover she is reporting from these cities I will immediately cease all travel.

Alex Fox
Lille, France

SIR — Some 25 years ago I set off for an impromptu visit to Paris. At Folkestone I found I had left my passport at home. I was advised that the French would not let me in, but that Belgium probably would. At Zeebrugge I was duly given a form to complete. This is what it said: "I — the undersigned — do hereby swear that I am the undersigned. In witness whereof I append my signature."

I was relieved and not a little amused to be permitted to enter. It seems less amusing now.

Christopher Macy
Wellingore, Lincolnshire

HOW TO FIGHT ISIL

SIR — Now that we have the telephone numbers of those recruited by ISIL can we just give the list to a telemarketing firm?

Philip J. Honey
Undy Caldicot, Monmouthshire

SIR — Emulating Boris Johnson's proposal that we refer to IS as *Daesh* perhaps the Far Left in British politics could change their favourite epithet from Tory Scum to Conservative Scum?

Philip Nierop
Whitestone, Devon

SIR – Ayatollah Khomeini famously said that there is no humour in Islam. The news that Saudi Arabia is to lead an international coalition against terrorism suggests otherwise.

Otto Inglis
Edinburgh

SIR – Surely the solution to ISIS is to declare that they are now part of the EU? Such a move would result in an instant end to their barbarity as they would be far too busy trying to determine how to deal with a raft of EU legislation.

Perhaps they could be offered the UK's position.

Stuart Mealing
London E8

THE HOUSE OF MIGRANTS

SIR – Should EU leaders set an example by converting the Strasbourg parliament building to permanent accommodation for refugee families? I'm sure the cost would be offset by the reduction in expenses in decamping from Brussels every other month.

Alan Kirk
Poole, Dorset

SIR – I'm afraid the hapless Angela Merkel has done the equivalent of advertising the party of the year on Facebook. She shouldn't be surprised when the Middle East and Africa turn up for the fun.

Stephen Webbe
East Molesey, Surrey

SIR – Having just seen the picture of Angela Merkel I switched on the television, which was showing a tribute to Bruce Springsteen. There she was again, larger than life at the piano.
  It turned out to be Elton John.

Geoff Milburn,
Glossop, Derbyshire

SIR – After spending 110 days over three and half years traveling around the UK on public transport – including a four-day stay in hospital – I have come to a conclusion: throw the whole lot out and keep the immigrants.

John Arthur Boyd
Lenham, Kent

THE FIRST GENTLEMAN

SIR – In expressing their condolences on Twitter at the passing of Nancy Reagan, President and Mrs Obama wrote as @POTUS and @FLOTUS.
  Should Mrs Clinton become president one wonders what acronym might be applied to Mr Clinton. HOTPUS perhaps?

Nicholas Lang
West Wickham, Greater London

SIR – Perhaps Bill Clinton will be known as the First Lady Killer.

Stephen Lawrence
Bratton, Wiltshire

BENITO TRUMP

SIR – Is it just me or does anyone else find that when Donald Trump purses his lips and pouts, he looks just like Benito Mussolini in his pomp?

I don't want to be a killjoy but look what happened to him. Donald might be well advised to keep away from piano manufacturers.

Michael Sheehy
Maidenhead, Berkshire

SIR – Is Donald Trump the Leicester City of American politics?

Peter Thompson
Sutton, Surrey

SIR – I am currently reading a collection of Alistair Cooke's *Letter from America*.

On February 23, 1990 he wrote: "Donald Trump, the young, bouncy, blond tycoon whose aspirations to take over hotels, casinos, airlines, resorts, cities — why not the country? — appear to be boundless".

What foresight!

Michael Thomas
Uffington, Oxfordshire

SIR — During the Cuban missile crisis of 1962, aged 11, I understood little of the detail but I recognised my parents' reactions and I was concerned. While parachute training when serving in the armed forces in 1971 I had confidence in the equipment and procedures but I was anxious. For the few seconds between losing control of the car and experiencing my first car accident in 1974 I was scared. When my cardiologist told me in 2013 that I had a blocked coronary artery I was frightened. Today I discovered that Donald Trump has a serious chance of becoming President of the USA and I'm bloody terrified.

David Mitchell
Aberdeen

SIR — If it happens I will invoke the title of the Anthony Newley musical: *Stop the world — I Want to Get Off*.

Clive Davidson
Worsley, Lancashire

SIR — Statue of Liberty according to Donald Trump:
Give me your tired, your poor,
Your huddled masses yearning to breathe free,
The wretched refuse of your teeming shore.
Send these, the homeless, tempest-tossed, to me:
I lift my lamp beside the golden door.
But as for Muslims? Please — no more.

Keith Davies
Telford, Shropshire

SIR – Donald Trump wants to prevent Muslims entering America. My experience is that it is quite difficult for white English Protestants in their seventies to enter America.

It is not a welcoming country.

Alan Hughes
Minster-on-Sea, Kent

SIR – Why ban Donald Trump from visiting Britain? With the pantomime season...

H.W.
Lesbury, Northumberland

SIR – If Donald Trump does come here, he must be made aware that the rodent he balances on his head will have to be quarantined for six months.

Geoff Smith
Gretna, Dumfriesshire

SIR – Donald Trump and Boris Johnson bring to mind a political jibe about the Wartime Minister of Information whose suitability for office was equally suspect: "Everything about you is a phoney. Even your hair which looks like a wig – isn't."

Adrian Bracken
Marbella, Spain

SIR – Please would the letters editor re-open the recent correspondence about neologisms, as I have just the one for Donald Trump: *Ignoranus*, a person who is at once thick and an a***hole.

Timothy Martin
London W1

SIR — After watching yet another speech with Donald Trump ranting and raving, saying anything to keep the headlines rolling, I was reminded of a football match from the late seventies which became a worldwide phenomenon.

A dog ran on the pitch, gained possession of the ball and, for a period of time, the game could not continue as the dog received all the attention.

Not wanting to look silly, none of the real players tried to get the ball back, so the mutt continued with his own game. Of course, he didn't score a goal as he didn't know where the goal was or indeed that the point was to score a goal in the first place. He just ran around with the ball making everyone dizzy until at last everyone got tired, including the dog.

Eventually the players got their ball back, the game resumed and the mutt was put in a kennel.

Come on, Mr Trump, roll over. There's a good boy. Give us the ball back.

Chris Handley
Wallsend, Tyne and Wear

SIR — I once went with my wife to a horse show in a small town in Iowa. As soon as we opened our British mouths three ladies wanted to know where we were from. One lady asked if we had come by train from England. Another remarked that we spoke English "real good". The third asked if we had always spoken English.

They were three delightful ladies and we got on fine with them, but sadly, their knowledge of the wider world was not great.

I now reflect that it is partly upon such people that the greatest democracy in the world is dependent for its presidential elections.

Sadly, one can easily uncover similar ignorance while electioneering in this country. I did so during the 2010 general election campaign.

Geoffrey Woollard
Soham, Cambridgeshire

SIR – As Her Majesty the Queen goes about her duties with evident relish she remains the best argument for a constitutional monarchy. Donald J. Trump is the second best.

Lt Col Patrick Chambers (retd)
Rosedale Abbey, North Yorkshire

ROYAL BLUSHES

'OW DO, HARRY?

SIR — You report that Prince Harry wants to have a quiet drink in a pub but can't.

Please send him my telephone number. Up here in the Derbyshire Dales there are plenty of cosy pubs serving great beer and food in wonderful surroundings, with landladies who will put the fear of God into any townie selfie-seekers.

The locals will bother him with little more than an "'Ow do?" We can sleep six, so his protection officers will be fine. My wife, however, may make them earn their keep.

Victor Launert
Matlock Bath, Derbyshire

SIR — I still quiver at the response I would expect from my old Regimental Sergeant Major if I had turned out in uniform with a facial growth (I can't call it a beard) like Prince Harry's. Amid the expletives would be the instruction to "Stand nearer to the razor."

Derek Lyon
Barrow in Furness, Cumbria

FLYING VISITS

SIR — Have other readers reflected on the Queen's extraordinary range of activities on July 13? The Court Circular tells us that she was in Cambridge in the morning, opening the East Anglian Air Ambulance Centre. Back in London Her Majesty accepted the resignation of one Prime Minister and appointed his successor. She then gave an audience to the Lord President before holding a council at 5.30pm.

Not bad going for a lady of 90.

Paul Fincham
Woodbridge, Suffolk

SIR — Visitors to our local beacon to celebrate the Queen's 90th birthday were given a sheet with the words of the first two verses of the National Anthem.

"We will only be singing the first verse," explained the helpful steward. "We don't have the music for the second."

N.H.
Worcester

SIR — Why did Her Majesty the Queen light a thousand beacons? Was Gondor calling for aid?

Mark Boyle
Johnstone, Renfrewshire

SIR — If the Queen reaches 100 years old, who will send her a congratulations card?

John Newman
Hinckley, Leicestershire

SIR — The Queen is lucky to be called Gan-Gan by Prince George. A friend of my daughter called her Grandmother Gaa-Gaa. A step too far, I thought.

Stephanie Cliffe
Staines-upon-Thames, Surrey

SPECIAL DELIVERY

SIR — The nation will be reassured by the news that two obstetricians and three midwives were on hand each time the Duchess of Cambridge gave birth, but what did the "four senior managers" actually do?

>**Dr John Doherty**
>Stratford-upon-Avon, Warwickshire

SIR — My wife read to me an article from *The Daily Telegraph* (while I was giving the cat its bath, before unplugging all the electrical sockets for the night) about Wills and Kate spending time in Norfolk so that Princess Charlotte will have as normal an upbringing as possible.

I am really glad. There seems to be an idea going round that people in Norfolk are unusual.

>**Terry Callan**
>Consdon, Norfolk

SIR — Presumably the recent gift of the home-made chutney from Katherine to the Queen could be regarded as a Duchess Original?

>**John Fletcher**
>Woodthorpe, Nottinghamshire

SIR — It seems churlish to criticise the Duke of Cambridge for carrying out too few duties while spending time with his young family when it's likely, if he follows his grandparents, that he will be working into his nineties.

>**Linda Johnson**
>West Lavington, Wiltshire

CHINESE WHISPERS

SIR – It is inevitable that the Queen, who is constantly monitored, should at some point make a comment she regrets. Rather than analysing this, shouldn't we be asking why were the Chinese "very rude"?

James Lloyd-Davies
London N20

SIR – David Cameron's overheard comments to the Queen regarding corruption in Nigeria and Afghanistan must be a great embarrassment to him. It's the first time in recent years that he has been heard telling the truth. He must be slipping.

Clive A. Smith
Stokeinteignhead, Devon

SIR – The bigger issue is why the Prime Minister had his hand in his trouser pocket while addressing Her Majesty.

Roger Moor
London NW9

SIR – The most shocking thing about the Buckingham Palace Garden Party revelations was that the Lord Chamberlain, William Peel, the 3rd Earl Peel, great-great-grandson of Prime Minister Sir Robert Peel, introduced a police officer to Her Majesty by saying, "Can I present?" instead of "May I present?"

Is the English language no longer a requirement for members of the Royal staff?

E.C. Coleman
Bishop Norton, Lincolnshire

LEXDEN'S LEXICON

SIR — The Queen has recently advertised for a senior correspondence officer. Does she have Lord Lexden in mind? His letters to *The Daily Telegraph* are always "timely and well composed", his knowledge of state affairs unsurpassed, and his pen is so prolific that I'd not be surprised if he couldn't oversee replies to the huge royal postbag in his spare time.

Peter Saunders
Salisbury, Wiltshire

DEAR
DAILY TELEGRAPH

BRAVO, PICTURE EDITOR

SIR — I have always admired the *Telegraph's* ability to picture scantily clad young ladies under the flimsiest of pretexts, but you have surpassed yourself with today's effort: "How to give your barbecue a Brazilian". While the three models in swimsuits and high heels, pictured clustered around an indeterminate burning object, had little relevance to the article on recipes, they filled a large proportion of the page delightfully. Bravo!

Charles Smith-Jones
Andover, Hampshire

SIR — I think there's a page missing from my paper — I can't find the photo of Helen Mirren.

John Waddington
Salisbury

SIR — I had to check that I had purchased the correct broadsheet yesterday. Inexplicably three of your models were smiling.

Henry Maj
Armitage, Staffordshire

SIR — Why is it that "celebrity" women, when having their photograph taken, insist on standing with their legs crossed as though they are in need of the loo? It does nothing to enhance their beauty and just makes them look ridiculous.

Anne Smith
Monikie, Angus

SIR — I really look forward to reading Michael Deacon's articles, but his photograph has always puzzled me. How could someone with that butter-wouldn't-melt expression write the way he does?

And then there he was in the Saturday magazine in all his glory: bearded (or unshaven), dark, mussy hair and a grumpy expression — absolutely wonderful. He was ranting about chocolate, cream eggs and this was the Michael Deacon I had always imagined.

Please, please change the photograph.

Eve Santler
Chester

SIR — I am baffled as to why you persist in including photographs of cast members of *The Archers* in your pages. My best guess is that they are for the benefit of the deaf, who will not know what the characters look like.

David Wells
London E6

SIR — Would time not be better spent on improving the acting and script-writing skills than on pictures of naked maturing ladies in an *Archers* calendar?

Please don't let my wife see this.

John Breining-Riches
Chagford, Devon

CROSS PURPOSES

SIR — I may be alone in this, but could I make a plea for a regular High Court gagging order puzzle. Having finished the *Telegraph* crossword, my wife and I spent an enjoyable hour or so trying to fill in the redacted Court Order for the latest celebrity scandal. Harmless fun for all the family.

Mike Morris
Stourbridge, West Midlands

SIR — A word of advice to all your crossword enthusiasts: do not pause for a sip of coffee while holding your pen in your drinking hand. I have just done so and poked myself in the eye.

David Brown
Lavenham, Suffolk

SIR — One of the pleasures of visiting my parents in Somerset was the rare opportunity to finish one or more cryptic crosswords together. We considered them tough but were determined. On this occasion, however, the pastime has become so arduous that I need a holiday to get over it.

Some clues are obtuse and others are downright twisted. One wonders if your target audience has become geniuses or disturbed.

P.M.
Wiveliscombe, Somerset

SIR — It is fully understood that puzzle setters are sadistic by nature but why do they insist on marking Killer Sudoku puzzles as "Gentle" when I know that it is going to be a nightmare?

Douglas Mumford
York

SIR – I have just successfully completed my first tough Sudoku. Stephen Hawking, ready when you are.

Paul Shippard
Oxshott, Surrey

SIR – Instead of labelling your puzzles moderate, tough, and so on, they must be given a puzzle equivalent calorie score (PECS).

This will enable us to decide whether it is better for our health to do the puzzle or go for a long walk instead.

D.J.J.
Horsham, West Sussex

SIR – I appreciate that cryptic crosswords are, by definition, devious, but I think last Saturday's Prize Crossword went beyond the pale by inferring that Tracy Emin is an artist.

A. Roberts
Dronfield, Derbyshire

TO PAGE 25 AND BEYOND

SIR – Why did Major Tim Peake go to the International Space Station to experience zero gravity when for £199.99 plus £9.95 delivery he could have picked up the Zero Gravity chair on special offer with the *Telegraph* on page 25 and experienced the same at home?

David Brinkman
Poole, Dorset

SIR – In Saturday's Travel section there was an advertisement for a two-week Mediterranean cruise costing £999 for a cabin. There was also a "free drinks package worth up to £1,150 per person".

Would you manage to find your way to the cabin?

Ralph Drew
Painswick, Gloucestershire

JOCULAR JUXTAPOSITION

SIR – A piece in today's *Telegraph* headlined: "Man, 74, collapses after Viagra tryst with woman, 27" is next to a story headed: "Bang goes a silent display."

Is it just me, or is the editor having a quiet laugh?

Gordon Garment
Chipping, Lancashire

CLASS ACTION

SIR – What on earth has happened to the class of your readership when your arts correspondent has to explain that White's is a Gentleman's club?

Perhaps she was subtly ensuring that the St. James's outpost was not confused with a similarly named and styled establishment, located on the outskirts of the City of London, where I am led to understand that young ladies from Lapland and Poland dance in order to earn funds to buy clothes.

Nicky Samengo-Turner
Gazeley, Suffolk

SIR – I shall cancel my subscription if **any** of your writers should ever again describe Ant and Dec as "everyone's best loved double-act".

Andrew Callaway
Northowram, West Yorkshire

HATCHES AND DISPATCHES

SIR – Sadly, we may have lost David Bowie but, according to your Birthday Column, Des O'Connor is still going strong at 84. Every cloud...

David Alsop
Churchdown, Gloucestershire

SIR – Following the recent deaths of such celebrated musicians as David Bowie, Glenn Frey and Dale Griffin, is God putting a band together?

Wendy May
Hereford

SIR – Today you have devoted a page to Charlie Sheen. I am happy and proud to have never heard of him. Had I been asked I would have guessed some sort of furniture polish.

Nigel Peacock
Llanbedr y Cennin, Conwy

SIR — Reading your Birthdays column I am repeatedly amazed to find that celebrities who were the same age as me during the 1980s and 1990s have now inexplicably become ten years younger. I wish I knew their secret.

Jill Smith
Stalbridge, Dorset

SIR — Anyone wanting their child to become an eminent future sports star would be well advised to take note of your Birthday column and plan accordingly: March 23 is the birthday of no fewer than eight people from diverse sports: Sir Roger Bannister, Jason Kenny, Wasim Bari, Sir Steve Redgrave, Mike Atherton, Joe Calzaghe, Sir Chris Hoy and Mo Farah.

Catherine Norton
Castleford, West Yorkshire

DISGUSTED OF CAMBRIDGE

SIR — I write out of concern for your editorial staff. On Saturday my 11-year-old daughter Lucy asked for the Sport supplement. Some ten minutes later I was subjected to a tirade of disgust arising from the total absence of any women's sport. Lucy finished the rout by pointing out that the only woman she could find was advertising a betting shop.

I have been on Lucy's bad side before and I don't recommend it to you. In your interests, would you consider a women's sport supplement once a month? I could then have my breakfast in peace and persuade Lucy to stand down.

J.S.
Cambridge

FRIENDS REUNITED

SIR – You published a letter from me on September 7. Next to my letter was one from a school friend I have not seen for over 50 years. Is this a new service being provided by *The Daily Telegraph*?

Andrew H.N. Gray
Edinburgh

SIR – I write to *The Daily Telegraph* a couple of times per week and friends call me an anorak. I point out to them that tens of thousands of people in Britain write to Facebook more than once a day.

Sir, imagine if your office had to deal with that lot.

Dave Alsop
Churchdown, Gloucestershire

SIR – I see *The Times* is advertising for readers to write letters to its editor. Do you have any spare ones you could send his way?

David Stanley
London SW6

SIR – I am worried not to have heard for a while from Les Sharpe, Hersham, Surrey, and Sandy Pratt, Dormansland, Surrey. Is all well with them? Maybe they should get together in times of writer's block.

If both horse racing fans they could meet at Sandown Park or Lingfield Park, which are close to their respective homes. A little fresh air and a flutter would possibly rejuvenate their jaded pens.

Concerned of Henfield.

Alyson Persson
Henfield, West Sussex

SIR:

> I keep writing to the Telegraph
> But I've fallen in the trap
> Of being too honest with my home address,
> (Which is) North of Watford Gap.
> Would the one who does the choosing
> Have a good look at a map.
> They'll see there are many places
> (To the) North of Watford Gap.
> On average only 1 in 16 letters
> That are chosen by the Telegraph chap
> To appear upon the letters page
> (Come from) North of Watford Gap.
> The other day on Radio 4
> I listened to your Editor chat.
> But you could tell that he had hardly been
> (Where?) North of Watford Gap.
> Give us a break, Letters Editor,
> We no longer wear shawls and a cap.
> Even the clogs are in decline
> (Up here) North of Watford Gap.
> Some of us have opinions
> And views that you should tap.
> Don't assume that all your readers
> (Reside) South of Watford Gap.

Alan Beresford
Chesterfield, Derbyshire (North of Watford Gap)

SIR — You printed two letters today from Malvern. Here's another one.

Malvern Harper
Ripley, Derbyshire

SIR — I forgot to put "SIR" at the head of my last letter. You are probably a woman anyway.
Sorry, sir.

Stefan Badham
Portsmouth

SIR — I must thank your correspondent Thomas W. Jefferson for helping me to understand why I have not been very successful over the past year in getting my letters published. Perhaps I should change my name to George Washington.

Professor M.M.R. Williams
Eastbourne, East Sussex

SIR — For months I have been sending you letters, but they are never published despite me having a double-barrelled name, retired officer rank and writing from the fashionable town of Whitstable.

Would it help if I provided a triple-barrelled name?

Lt Col Alistair St John-Grahame-Stewart (retd)
Formerly Alistair St John-Grahame
Whitstable, Kent

SIR — Demonstrating the great meritocracy that is the *Telegraph* letters page my prenominal is seemingly of no use when writing to you. With none published my ambition is undiminished.

Once in my first year as a professor at a north-east university it was politely explained to me — across a large committee — that my role now was simply to sit there and raise my eyebrows once in a while. Do nothing vocal, offer nothing critical. Wait until the *Telegraph* hears about this, I thought.

Professor Craig Richardson
Taston, Oxfordshire

SIR — Our postman, whom I'd never met before today, told me that he'd seen my recent contribution to your Letters page.
    "Concise and pithy".
    Just like this one.

John H. Stephen
London NW8

SIR — While considering whether to buy your unpublished letters book I have been dismayed to read Iain Hollingshead's otherwise encouraging piece which tells us that you have received none from Tunbridge Wells this year. I alone have sent you six since January 1, all of which were automatically acknowledged.

Most were quite good, certainly deserving a place in your new book, if not in the paper.

In the hope that this one might actually be read and Tunbridge Wells regain pride of place in your letter columns.

I am Yours disgustedly,

Donald Clarke
Tunbridge Wells, Kent

SIR – Have you thought of producing a book of the letters by Stan Eckersley of Pudsey and Graham Hoyle of Baildon? You could entitle it "Letters on Every Subject from West Yorkshire".

Patricia Hargreaves
Guiseley, West Yorkshire

STILL ALONE IN THINKING

SIR – You may like to know that, two years since the publication of my unpublished letter in the admirable book *What Will They Think of Next...?*, I have still not received a reply to my request to the captains of two major food retailers on how to open shrink-wrapped food without damaging the contents.

Should I let you know in another two years?

Terry Burke
Canterbury, Kent

THE DAILY STROKE

SIR – This morning, on offering the *Telegraph* to my wife, she replied: "Not yet; I think I'll take my blood pressure first."

Dr A.E. Hanwell
York

SIR – The only thing to raise my spirits in these times of turmoil has been Matt.

Penelope Escombe
Brigstock, Northamptonshire

P.S.

P.S.

Dear Iain,

Well, now, there I was reading Henry Pelling's excellent biography of Winston Churchill — in awe of how the dashing young cavalryman managed to send reports to The Daily Telegraph between death-defying skirmishes on the North-West Frontier — and up steps the postman with your letter telling me that one of my own Daily Telegraph "reports", sent from the comparatively safe enclave of Edenbridge, is to be published in your book.

Could it possibly be the letter about the mystery of how the washing-up gets done at Downton Abbey? I thought it might stand a chance, being a subject of universal curiosity to those of us who spend hours chained to the sink listening to Radio 4.

I will, of course, be buying a copy of your book and advising the small but exclusive circle of people invited to my funeral to do likewise.

Best wishes,

Robert Cox

Dear Iain,

I was thrilled to get your letter.

I will be a published author: so much better to have a letter in your book than in a throwaway newspaper.

As a child, like all of us, I couldn't wait for Christmas; the feeling has returned.

Thank you.

Greig Bannerman

Dear Mr Hollingshead,
I would be honoured to have one of my letters included. Or perhaps I should say:

SIR – After years of waiting for recognition for all my voluntary work etc. I have hit the jackpot. Forget your honours list, Mr Cameron; I've had a letter from Mr Iain Hollingshead.
Kind regards

Sheelagh James

Dear Iain – if I may!
I was delighted to receive your letter and am chuffed that you have chosen to print another letter of mine in one of your volumes. Most certainly I agree to its printing. Vanity forbids otherwise.

I had been thinking about future titles for your books. I offer the following as a suggestion: Say What You Like, but...
Do feel free if the mood takes you.
All good wishes,

Edward Thomas